*The
Ivy
Book*

The Ivy Book

The Growing and Care of Ivy and Ivy Topiary

SUZANNE PIEROT

Photographs by Michael Mullally

Macmillan Publishing Co., Inc.

NEW YORK

Collier Macmillan Publishers

LONDON

Macmillan Publishing Co., Inc.
866 Third Avenue, New York, N.Y. 10022
Collier-Macmillan Canada Ltd.

Library of Congress Catalog Card Number: 73–1855

First Printing 1974

Printed in the United States of America

This, too, is for Jacques

Contents

Acknowledgments   ix

1. *Ivy Is Ivy Is Ivy—Or Is It?*   1

2. *Ivy's Shady History*   5

3. *Ivy Culture, or All That's Needed
Is a Little Love*   13

4. *The Nitty Gritty About Ivy, or the
Botanist's Eye-view of Hedera*   22

5. *Bird's Foot Ivies*   31

6. *The Fans*   45

7. *The Curlies*   53

8. *The Variegateds*   67

9. *The Heart Shapes* 83

10. *The Ivy-Ivies* 91

11. *Miniatures* 99

12. *Hardy Outdoor Ivy* 109

13. *The Oddities* 119

14. *Starter's Collection* 131

15. *"Ivy" That Isn't Ivy* 132

16. *Topiary—Fun and Art* 137

Suppliers 156

Index 157

Acknowledgments

WHEN MY friend Carolyn Koch complained to me that she could not find a nurseryman who could verify the correct name for her ivy plants, she sowed the idea for a book about ivy. Now, five years later, I hope she will find the answers she wants in these pages.

I thank Sylvia Dowling, not only for working with me on this book, but for her untiring patience in helping me sort through the many varieties of ivy to select the ones finally chosen for inclusion. We experimented together with plants grown in my home in New York and in hers in Connecticut. There were days we became discouraged when we searched for a new word for a shade of green. Olive? Leaf? Spinach? Drab? Bouncy? Money? Girl Scout?

Michael Mullally not only took the extraordinary pictures for the book, but to do so had to design and build a new type of photographic table made of translucent glass with floodlights and spotlights above and below the plant. Such strong light made the close-up pictures possible—but it also killed half the plants.

A special thank you, too, to Al Califano who worked with Mullally in perfecting the development of the pictures The two of them work by day making television commercials and on occasion would work all night, too, developing the ivy pictures.

But most of all, I would like to thank my husband Jacques Pierot III not only for his editing but for his encouragement and understanding.

*The
Ivy
Book*

I.
Ivy Is Ivy
Is Ivy—
Or Is It?

Ivy is the practical joker of the plant world. A gracefully elegant mischievous beauty of a plant that seems to delight in baffling the botanists in their efforts to straighten out the tangled nomenclature of its many forms. It's easy to tell that an ivy is an ivy. The trick is to know what *kind* of ivy it is. Even the acknowledged *experts* can't always agree on identification.

The problem of identifying the many kinds of ivy has been with us since Nero wore a wreath of it around his head, fiddling while Rome burned. The reason is simple: The only available clues are the shape, size, veins, and different colors of the leaves; and with only these clues, determination is difficult since older and younger leaves on the *same stem* may look different.

The problem is actually even more complicated. If three different people bought the same kind of ivy, on the same day, from the same nursery—six months later their plants could look like three different kinds of ivy because of the

1

different environments they were put in and the different amounts of sunlight, water, and food they received. What's more, not one of the horticultural varieties of ivy grows true from seed. Adding to this botanical bewilderment is the carefree and very confusing way the ivy itself chooses to grow. You may have a beautiful, healthy, marvelous-looking ivy plant with all the leaves looking pretty much alike, then suddenly a new kind of leaf or shoot will show up. If you propagate that leaf or shoot, chances are you'll get an ivy that is completely different from the parent plant. Shoots such as these are called *sports*. Ivy's tendency to produce a shoot, or sport, with leaves different from the mother plant usually occurs when life has been good to the plant; it often happens in a greenhouse.

When a nurseryman sees a sport with an especially new and different kind of leaf shape, he is usually quick to propagate it. He gives the sport a new name, sends it all over the country, and then, more often than not, it "sports" back to one of its primitive forms. Many a sport has made "bad sports" of ivy fanciers because many of the trade names given to supposedly new discoveries are local names of the sports.

Compounding the confusion resulting from this impish ivy is the fact that there are several different kinds of sports. There is the *bud* sport, which comes from the tip of the juvenile foliage and is the rascal that refuses to produce the plant it came from when propagated from a cutting. Another is called the *intermediate* sport, which shoots up when the plant is between its adult and juvenile stage. These sports are the prolific ones, and each is different from the other.

Yet, as different as each ivy plant looks, all of them came from just five species. This intriguing fact makes ivy fun to grow and keep as a guest in your home or garden because there's never a dull moment with it.

And that's why so much space is devoted in this book to life-size, close-up photographs of as many ivies as possible,

The ivy in this book is organized into nine categories:

Outdoor or hardy
Variegateds or multicolored ivies
Curly-edged ivies
Bird's Foot-shaped ivies
Heart-shaped ivies
Fan-shaped ivies
Hardy ivy that will survive outdoors
The Oddities
"Ivy" ivies—the classics

After you read this book, you'll be probably the first on your block, or in your club, or even in your town to speak with some authority on ivy. There's hardly anybody who can.

Napoleon Ivy

A TRADITIONAL PATTERN OF HISTORICAL INTEREST. NAPOLEON IVY WAS SUPPLIED FOR THE USE OF THE EX-EMPEROR NAPOLEON BONAPARTE WHEN HE WAS EXILED TO THE ISLAND OF ST. HELENA IN 1815. THE GREEN AND BROWN PATTERN IS ON FINE EARTHENWARE TRADITIONAL SHAPES.

2.
Ivy's Shady History

IVY STARTED OUT as an emblem of virtue, prosperity, and beneficence; but somewhere along the line it got mixed up with the licentious orgies of Bacchus. There is a happy ending: Like its habit of growing, ivy was able to rise above its surroundings and any bad reputation it ever had.

Ivy has been eulogized by poets (Horace, Vergil, Chaucer, Dryden, Dickens, et al.); glorified by artists (Wedgwood); symbolized by craftsmen (Hitchcock); etched in glass (Lalique); plasticized by merchants (Woolworth); and even embodied in academic form by college students (the Ivy League). No wonder the ivy has a sense of humor.

It isn't easy to trace ivy's historical growth with any degree of accuracy (and without laughing a lot), but it is known that one of the chief deities of Egypt, Osiris, who gave his people their knowledge of agriculture, adopted ivy as a symbol of his benefactions to mankind. Ivy in the Egyptian language was called *Chen-Osiris*, "the plant of Osiris." The ivy-wreathed thyrus, a long rod or wand, became the symbol of Osiris. But like everything else that starts out with noble motives, Osiris's rod became a lethal weapon in some situations. It was not unusual for someone to hide a spear under the ivy leaves and for the spear-bearer to take some unneighborly jabs at his neighbors.

Meanwhile, back in Greece, there was a god by the name of Dionysus. He was the Olympian god of nature (sometimes known as the God of the vine—or wine). In Rome the same god was called Bacchus. Bacchus had a great admiration for Osiris, and in an effort to honor him, he adopted the ivy for his own brand of worship. Some scholars have concluded that Bacchus's worship of ivy was because it reputedly modified the intoxicating effect of wine—a rather foolish and unrealistic conclusion, I think. Why would Bacchus and his followers, who liked nothing better than the juice of the grape, want to weaken its effect and slow down the orgies associated with it?

If you study the drawings and paintings of the bacchanalian feasts, you'll see many of the guests with wreaths or garlands of ivy draped around their heads. Maybe a little askew but, nevertheless on their heads.

Pliny the Elder, a Roman naturalist (A.D. 23–79), who made a study of the various kinds of ivies, claims that Bacchus was the first to use garlands and that ivy was the leaf that was used.

Vergil, in his fifth Pastoral, poetically reported that ivy was used even in the memorials to Bacchus. Daphnis, the shepherd, was not only a lover of some note, but according to Vergil:

Fierce tigers Daphnis taught the yoke to bear;
And first with curling ivy dressed the spear.
Daphnis did rites to Bacchus first ordain;
And holy revels for his reeling train.

Ivy was a favorite with poets throughout the centuries, but it received scant biblical notice. Though not mentioned by name in the Bible, ivy formed "the corruptible crown" for which the athletes at the Isthmian games contended. Ivy is mentioned in the book of Maccabees:

> And in the day of the king's birth, every month they were brought by bitter constraint to eat of the sacrifices; and when the feast of Bacchus was kept, the Jews were compelled to go in procession to Bacchus, carrying Ivy.

Ivy's historical background is as intriguing and varied as its method of growing. Ivy found its way into the Christian world; in their celebrations of Jesus' birth, the early Christians used ivy in their garlands. Even the old English carols gave ivy a place of honor:

> Holly hat berys as red as any Rose
> The foster the hunters, kepe hem from the doo.
>> Nay, Ivy! Nay, hyt, shall not.

> Ivy hat berys as black as any slo:
> There com the oule and ete him as she go.
>> Nay, Ivy! Nay, hyt, shall not.

Though ivy did enjoy a modicum of respectability, it couldn't quite shake its association with Bacchus. Ivy was used in probably the very first sign made to advertise a saloon. "The sign of the bush" over a doorway, or even in front of a tent, meant that good cheer was available inside. The sign was a pole with a bunch of green leaves tied to the end of it, and the leaves were usually ivy. Chaucer called the pole an "alestake":

> A garland hadde he sette up on his hede
> As gret as it were for an alestake.

Most people called it an "alepole," and most inns used it as their only sign. Eventually, the better bars adopted ivy in their names. "The Ivy Bush," "The Ivy Green," "Ivy Inn" were a few of them. As time went on and tastes improved (decorative tastes, that is), the more elegant bistros announced their goodies to the world by simply displaying a painting of Bacchus sitting on a cask with a wreath of ivy leaves around his head.

But it was the poets who gave ivy a place of honor. Horace, the lyric poet of his day (circa 65 B.C.), considered ivy worthy enough to be associated with his benefactor Maecenas:

> An ivy-wreath, fair learning's prize,
> Raises Maecenas to the skies.

Byron described ivy as "the garland of eternity." Wordsworth and Keats identified it with the majesty of maturity:

> Grey locks profusely round his temples hung
> In clustering curls, like ivy, which the bite
> of winter cannot thin . . .
> —"The Excursion," Wordsworth

> His aged head, crown's with beechen wreath,
> Seem'd like a poll of ivy in the teeth
> Of Winter hoar.
> —"Endymion," Keats

Shakespeare mentioned ivy at least four times, but it was Charles Dickens who wrote the most charming tribute in "The Ivy Green":

Oh a dainty plant is the Ivy green,
 that creepeth o'er ruins old!
Of right choice food are his meals I ween,
 In his cell so lone and cold.
The wall must be crumbled, the stone decayed,
 To pleasure his dainty whim;
And the mouldering dust that years have made,
 Is a merry meal for him.
  Creeping where no life is seen,
  A rare old plant is the Ivy green.

Fast he stealeth on, though he wears no wings
 And a staunch old heart has he.
How closely he twineth, how tight he clings,
 to his friend the huge Oak Tree!
And slily he traileth along the ground,
 And his leaves he gently waves,
As he joyously hugs and crawleth round
 The rich mould of dead men's graves.
  Creeping where grim death is seen,
  A rare old plant is the Ivy green.

Whole ages have fled and their works decay'd,
 And nations have scatter'd been;
But the stout old Ivy shall never fade,
 From its hale and hearty green.
The brave old plant in its lonely days
 Shall fatten upon the past;
For the stateliest building man can raise
 Is the Ivy's food at last.
  Creeping on where time has been
  A rare old plant is the Ivy green.

Ivy has been accused of possessing the habits and vices
of a vampire and living off the blood of aged and decrepit

buildings. Yet, it has kept many a wall standing by absorbing the dampness that threatened to make the wall crumble and decay. I am convinced that many a stately home in England, and many a neglected medieval building, remains standing today because ivy chose centuries ago to throw a resplendent green mantle of glossy protection over it.

Of course, ivy does loosen mortar. It does get under clapboards. It can be destructive and must be kept in check on some buildings. But, for instant age and that "old world" look, nothing surpasses it. All you need is the money for repairs.

Through the centuries there have been many people who have accused ivy of strangling trees in its determination to cover everything it touches. But ivy is not a parasite. Parasites do not produce green leaves or manufacture chlorophyll. The ivy does not sap the energies of a tree to live. It does not need the tree's nutriment. It certainly gets no nourishment from a stone wall; yet it thrives as much on a lifeless wall as it does on a tree.

Jefferson grew ivy at Monticello, but it was not a native plant. This was borne out by several books written in the eighteenth and nineteenth centuries and even in the writings of Captain John Smith (of Pocahontas fame) back in 1624. In "Virginia, the generalle historie of Virginia, New England and the Summer Isles," the good Captain wrote "The poysoned weed is much in shape like our English ivy."

In a book called *Travels in North America*, written by Peter Kalm and published in 1748, the author relates:

Near the town [Philadelphia], I saw an ivy or *Hedera helix*, planted against the wall of a stone building which was so covered by the fine green leaves of this plant as almost to conceal the whole. It was doubtless brought over from Europe for I have never perceived it anywhere else in my travels through North America.

"A Treatise on the Theory and Practice of Landscape Gardening adapted to North America" written by Andrew Jackson Downing and published by Wiley and Putman (New York) in 1844, states:

The Ivy is not a native of America; nor is it by any means a very common plant in our gardens, though we know of no apology for the apparent neglect of so beautiful a climber . . . One of the most beautiful growths of this plant, which has ever met our eyes, is that upon the old mansion in the Botanic Garden at Philadelphia. . . .

It was in the 1870s, shortly after the Civil War, that ivy got a firm hold in the United States. Ocean travel for many Americans was becoming popular, and outdoor photography was coming into its own. Travelers returning from England brought back many pictures of ivy-covered buildings, especially castles and old manor houses. In America, ivy was so treasured that it was grown in pots and used as a living frame around doorways, windows, mirrors, and paintings. A big fad was indoor screens completely covered with growing ivy. Soon it became the favorite decorating motif for furniture, dinnerware, glassware, wallpaper, and many objets d'art. It still is.

A person can go to Tiffany's in New York and buy an ivy-decorated dinner plate made by Wedgwood for about fifteen or twenty dollars and then walk down the street to the first five-and-ten-cent store and find the same design on a plastic ruffle for shelf edging.

From Bacchus to Woolworth, ivy has had quite a life.

3.

Ivy Culture

or All That's Needed
Is a Little Love

How MANY TIMES have you visited a well-kept, attractive home and noticed a pitiful ivy in a pot struggling for its life? Sure, it has leaves. And they're green. But the wide gaps where leaves once flourished are mute testimony to sad neglect.

If you do what no nice guest would do and peek into the pot, you'd probably find the soil dry and parched, cracked and crumbling. If your hostess, who probably spends hours every week fussing with her hair or nails, had devoted just a few minutes of attention to her potted friend, she could have been rewarded with a green, lush, fully leafed oasis of gracefulness.

It's so easy to turn ivy into an exciting showpiece that your friends can ooh and ahh over when they see it in your home. Not much needs to be done. You need to observe only a few simple rules to steer that middle course between coddling and utter neglect—that's one of the joys of raising ivy.

13

Soil

Ivy isn't fussy about soil as long as it has good drainage. Of course, a rich, organic soil will produce faster and thicker growth, but it isn't vital. In fact, variegated ivies should be grown in poor soil to stimulate the growth of colored foliage. If you give the variegateds too much food, the leaves will be mainly green.

To get good drainage in ordinary soil, mix a little perlite in it. Perlite is probably one of the greatest soil aids ever created. The little white granules are pretty, too. You may also mix a little vermiculite in the soil. Many people find that vermiculite retains too much water, especially when watering is done with a heavy hand. Vermiculite is acceptable if you're not a compulsive waterer.

Peat moss and milled spaghnum are also excellent soil additives. The important thing is that whatever the soil, you must keep it moist—not soggy.

Many people have the erroneous impression that ivy requires a very acid soil—not so. A pH of 6.0 to 7.0 is ideal, and unless your soil comes from the deep woods (where it is very acid) or if you happen to live on a limestone rock (which is alkaline), chances are your soil is absolutely perfect for ivy. If you want to be really accurate and have fun too, you can buy a soil-testing kit at any garden-supply store. These kits are inexpensive and easy to use.

What does pH mean? It's really quite simple. A soil's pH is a measurement of its *hydrogen ion concentration*. The pH scale reads from 1 to 14; 7 is neutral and readings above that point mean that the soil is alkaline. For instance, if your soil has a pH 7.8 you may be sure it is on the alkaline side. The higher the number above 7, such as pH 7.8 or 8.0, the greater the alkalinity of your soil. If the figure is below 7, the soil will tend to be acid. The lower the number is below 7, such as pH 6.5, 6.0, or 5.0, the higher the acidity of your soil.

The most satisfactory pH for a garden soil in which many different plants can be grown (including ivy) is between pH 6.5 and pH 7.0. A pH 8.0 shows signs of severe mineral deficiency and would starve your plants. The soil should be carefully fed until the requisite pH is acquired.

When growing ivy outdoors, simply make sure the soil is good garden loam with adequate drainage. To get professional help at no cost, send a sample of your soil in a small plastic bag to the Agricultural Extension Station in your state.

Fertilizer

For indoor ivy any "balanced" fertilizer such as 10–10–10 or 15–15–15 is excellent. A fertilizer is balanced when the three numbers in the formula are the same. Those three numbers stand for the amount of nitrogen, phosphoric acid, and potash in the formula, and in that order. (An unbalanced fertilizer, such as 15–30–15, is used for flowering plants.)

There are many good brands of fertilizer on the market such as Peters, Rapid-Gro, and Miracle-Gro. All these brands indicate their formula on the label.

Unless they are variegated ivies, fertilize your plants every other week, or at least once a month. I remind myself on the first and fifteenth of the month that it is fertilizer time, but if you should miss a date, don't worry.

Ivy is always grateful for any kindness bestowed on it and forgives an occasional lapse.

When ivy is used as a ground cover, plant it in a well-prepared soil, mulched with hay to prevent washing-out and weed growth. Space plants one foot apart in each direction. In this case, you can lime, if necessary, and fertilize the soil before applying the hay.

In establishing the ground-cover planting, two fertilizations, one at time of planting and another two months later, are desirable. Usually two to three pounds of 10–10–10 fertilizer per 100 square feet is ideal. Once this is established, fertilize infrequently because over stimulation tends to soften the stems and make the plants susceptible to winter kill.

When fertilizing topiaries, it is a good idea to put liquid fertilizer in a spray bottle and spray directly on the leaves, in addition to pouring it onto the soil.

Watering

The most important aspect of caring for ivy is the simplest—watering. Ivy thrives in moist soil. *Moist*, I said, not soggy. If you want to show your ivy the absolute in affection, you will put it in the sink once in a while and give it a brisk shower. This not only keeps the leaves clean and shiny, but it will also help get rid of any spider mites that might be lurking underneath the leaves.

If you have a grafted plant lay the plant on its side and spray; don't set it erect until all excess water has drained from it. The weight of the top growth plus the added weight of the excess water can be enough to pull the grafts right out of their sockets.

Ivy would rather be kept in a humid room. If you don't

care to live that way, simply set the plant on a tray with wet pebbles or damp peat moss and your ivy will be perfectly content.

It is remarkable how many novices believe that ivy should be kept soaking wet. Possibly this is because cut vines of almost any ivy root readily and grow in water, however ivy in a pot will not tolerate a soggy soil. Good drainage and a humid atmosphere are its beauty secrets.

The eminent horticulturalist Alfred Bates related an interesting story of his experience with watering:

> The first thing I found out about the nature of the Ivy was the very great difference that the amount of moisture in the soil had upon it; causing so great an increase in the size of the leaf and in the distance between nodes as to completely change the appearance of the plant. Years ago three cuttings were got from a very small leaved, dark green variety of which I am still uncertain as to the name; after they were rooted one was planted in almost full shade where the ground was only comparatively moist, the second was planted below a low stone edging in almost full sun but where water stood for some time after every rain and the third was grown in a pot where it was given regular and copious watering. The last two grew luxuriously until they approached the variety gracilis both in leaf and inter-node while the first, that in the drier soil, has still retained its small leaf and its rather short inter-node. It has slowly climbed up an old grape arbor post until now that it has reached the top and is beginning to send out stems which search for more support I hope that I may be able to obtain it in an arborescent form." *

* Alfred Bates, "The Illusive Ivy," *National Horticulture Magazine*, January 1932.

When ivy is being trained to grow either as a topiary or on some kind of wire form, such as described in chapter 16, it must be sprayed regularly with water. Ivy is a most agreeable plant, but if you are making it into a showpiece topiary you are also transforming it into a prima donna. You must therefore treat it like a prima donna and spray it at least once a day, preferably twice.

The Bronx Sprayer (available at garden-supply centers) is probably one of the best of all sprayers. However if you are inclined to be lazy, as well as economical, save all your hair-setting-lotion bottles or any detergent bottle that comes with a spray top. (Get-set, Windex, Fantastic, to name a few.) Leave one next to each topiary, and then whenever you pass by, it will be easy to give the plant a little spraying.

Larger topiaries, such as a 3-foot-tall flamingo I once made, demand about a gallon of water daily. The flamingo sat beside my water-lily pool and every time I passed it, I poured the entire watering can over it. The water drippings fell into the pool. That's something to remember when you bring your topiaries into the house for the winter. Place them where water drippings won't do any damage, or be prepared to mop.

Light

Ivies will tolerate far more sun than most people realize, except that under full sunlight they grow considerably slower Ivy, by nature, is a shade-loving plant, but it certainly will grow in full sun. What is dangerous about planting it in full sun is that the winter sun will do more harm to it than the winter cold. Except for the tender species, ivies take more kindly to frost or a light freeze than they do to the dry heat of a room or the harsh rays of a winter sun.

Diseases and Insects

Ivy doesn't usually tell you it's sick. So, if you don't give it a checkup once in a while, you'll never know until it's too late.

SCALE   Every so often, lift a few leaves and look for scattered brown bumps stuck underneath. If you see any, it means your ivy has scale. These insects are almost invisible, and that's when they're doing the most damage. It is not until they form their hard scale-like shell that they are visible. Spray over and under leaves with Malathion, mixed according to package directions.

MITES   Mites are common on ivy, especially during hot and dry seasons or if kept in a moistureless room. These pests are hard to see without a magnifying glass, but their damage resembles tiny, grey needle-like specks on the leaves. Spray with Malathion or Kelthane.

RED SPIDER   These are tiny eight-legged mites that live on the underside of leaves and can be seen with a hand lens. They suck the sap of the leaf and cause speckling and discoloration of the leaves. Spray with Malathion or Blackleaf 40.

LEAF SPOT Ivy can get leaf spot and aphids, although neither are common. Leaf spot causes one-quarter-inch brown spots that appear on the underside of the leaf and often come through to the top. If you should see it, pick off and burn damaged leaves. Ivy grown in full sun where heat is intense is more susceptible to leaf spot. Spray with a fungicide containing copper or use Bordeaux Mixture.

APHIDS Aphids, as you probably know, are soft-bodied, tiny insects that suck sap from the plant. Spray with Malathion or Lindane.

ANTHRACNOSE Symptoms of Anthracnose are black spots on the leaf and stem. Spray with a fungicide containing copper or use Bordeaux Mixture.

Propagation

Outdoors or indoors, ivy is a joy to propagate. When I lived in Stamford, Connecticut, I had a stone retaining wall around an island in the middle of the Rippowam River. The wall looked bare, and I wanted it softened with the gracefulness of ivy. Instead of making a lot of little cuttings, I pulled the long strands from some ivy I had growing in abundance in another section of the garden. The strands that had a root at one end must have been at least twenty feet long.

I simply planted the root and laid the full twenty feet in the soil along the edge of the wall. I planted one strand after the other until the wall was encircled. Then, between each cluster of leaves, I covered the vine with soil. It wasn't long before each cluster of leaves had become a new plant of ivy and magnificently cascaded over the wall into the river.

Often, long strands of ivy trailing on the ground root themselves this way naturally. This is called *layering*. To make cuttings from layered plants, cut off vines where they have rooted and replant.

You can also take tip cuttings by snipping the ends of trailing vines and putting them in water. Remove any leaves that would be covered with water. In a short time these plants will have sufficient roots for use in containers of water. Ivy that is rooted in water does not transplant well into soil. If you want to grow them in soil, root your cuttings in moist vermiculite mixed with sand or perlite for drainage.

To root cuttings, remove the bottom leaf or leaves and insert the cuttings in rows in a flat or pot of vermiculite and sand, or a mixture of vermiculite and perlite. Keep the flat or pot moist and shaded until fresh new leaves form, which indicates that the roots are growing and have taken hold. Another way is to give a gentle tug to the cutting—very gentle—and if there is a little resistance, you'll know the roots have formed.

4.
The Nutty Gritty About Ivy

or The Botanist's Eye-view of Hedera

THE PURPOSE of this book is to help you understand a rather complex plant in a simple and agreeable manner. If you are interested in delving a little deeper into the peculiarities of ivy, this chapter should serve that purpose. On the other hand, if diagnosing variants and probing foliage differences is not your cup of tea, then you may just as well skip this chapter. All the information you need for identifying the myriad ivy varieties as well as growing beautiful lush plants and topiaries is in the chapters ahead.

Ivy's botanical name is *Hedera* (hed'-er-a), and it belongs to the *Araliaceae* family. *Hedera* is its classical name, and the origin is Latin. Ivy is described by botanists as a climbing or scandent wood plant that becomes shrublike or treeform at maturity. The two steps are, for the most part, distinct. In their juvenile stage of development all ivies have climbing stems supported by aerial rootlets that are present in varying degrees of abundance. At this stage the plants do not flower. In the adult stage, when the plant becomes shrubby, the ivy has no aerial rootlets, and the climbing tendency disappears. It flowers and bears fruit. But, with the exception of "238th Street," this rarely happens in the colder northern climates.

The juvenile stage has ended and the adult stage has begun when you find an erect ascending branch without aerial rootlets and with unfamiliar foliage. It is on these branches that the flower and fruits are borne. These fruits, which look like little berries, are poisonous.

Juvenile leaves on the same plant can have an entirely different shape and size than the adult leaves, or from each other. They can even have a different number of lobes or no lobes at all. The younger leaves are of lighter color than the older leaves, but don't be surprised to find that some of the older leaves are smaller than some of the younger.

It is almost impossible to tell the variety the adult leaves originated from if the cutting is taken away from the plant. Botanists can identify species of ivy by the character of "hairs" on the lowerside of the foliage and on the stalks of the fruit, which are so small one needs a strong magnifying lens to see them and a microscope to identify them.

There are five species of Hedera in cultivation, and they can be identified most easily in their juvenile stage. The ivy most often grown is *Hedera helix* and there are over 100 varieties grown in the United States. The other four species have only a few varieties. The five species are:

Hedera helix   *Hedera colchica*
Hedera carnariensis   *Hedera nepalensis*
              Hedera rhombea

Hedera Helix: English Ivy

This is the species you find most frequently in America and Western Europe, both cultivated and naturalized. (The English prefer to call it "The Ivy.") It is hardy in most parts of the United States. Two of the most popular outdoor varieties are hibernica and baltica, and of these two varieties, baltica is probably the most hardy.

The varieties and clones of *Hedera helix* can be distinguished by their juvenile foliage, which is dark green and has whitish veins. The leathery leaves are from one to three inches long or longer, usually five-lobed with heart-shaped bases. The hairs seen through a microscope, have four to six rays. Stems are dull green to purplish.

In the adult stage the foliage is uniformly olive-green without the whitish veins. The flowers are greenish yellow, the fruit black or yellowish orange. Clones of *Hedera helix* number in the hundreds. Fortunately they fall into three groups.

GROUP ONE: The self-branching ivies. This group produces an abundance of lateral branchees along the ends of the stems in the leaf axils. Included in this group are 'Merion Beauty', 'Maple Queen', and 'Meagheri'.

GROUP TWO: These are ivies that are long and trailing and do not branch profusely, although some varieties may have an occasional lateral branch. The leaves are uniformly green in summer and tinted reddish purple in winter. *Helix* in group two include 'Erecta', 'Conglomerata', 'Curlilocks', 'Manda's Crested', 'Telecurl', 'Pedata', 'Sagittaefolia', baltica *, 'Walthamensis', hibernica.*

* These are botanical varieties, and although propagated as clones they can be found in the wild. The variety baltica is known as Baltic ivy. Hibernica is known as Irish ivy.

GROUP THREE: The variegated ivies. These are in a separate group because of their coloring, but their growing habit can be either self-branching or long and trailing. They include 'Goldust', 'Green Quartz', 'Goldheart', and 'Heise Denmark'.

Less is known about the origins of group two than about the other two groups. Groups one and three have been known for more than a century. Most of them are of British origin.

Hedera Canariensis: Canary Island Ivy

This species, the darling of the florists, is a native of North Africa and is grown outdoors all over the West Coast of the United States. Most of the large-leafed variegated ivies belong to this species, and while they are not reliably hardy outdoors, except on the West Coast and in the South, they do make spectacular house plants. An ivy expert, Mrs. Arthur Michaels of Rye, New York, grows her *Hedera canariensis* in a protected spot under a covering of pine needles that fall naturally from the trees above. I would be afraid to grow it farther north than southern Connecticut.

Hedera canariensis is the only ivy species that produces bright burgundy-red twigs and leaf stems. Its leaves are large (seven or eight inches across) glossy, and more apple-green in color than you find in the other species. Its hairs are grayish white with about fifteen rays, which tend occasionally to be star shaped. Juvenile leaves commence egg shaped, then become triangular and unlobed. During growth they develop from three to five lobes. In the adult stage (depending on the climate, it can take many years) the leaves become egg shaped again although slightly thicker and less glossy than in their juvenile stage.

Its fruit is black and the size of a pea. Varieties of *Hedera canariensis* include 'Canary Cream', 'Variegata', and 'Margino-maculata.'

Hedera Colchica: Persian Ivy

A native of most of Asia and Southeastern Europe, *Hedera colchica* can be fairly easily identified by its rather thick, leathery, heart-shaped, pointed leaves and dull, dark green color. Crush the leaves and they smell like celery! The stems are a pea-green and very scaly. *Colchica's* hair is yellow with about eighteen to thirty rays. The leaves of the juvenile foliage are broadly egg shaped and occasionally three-lobed. On the lowerside of the leaves the surface is ribbed. The veins on the upperside of the leaf are ribbed near the base and gradually become depressed across the rest of the surface. The adult foliage does not differ from the juvenile foliage to any great extent except that it is narrower and, of course, the leaves do not have any lobes. *Hedera colchica's* pea-sized fruit is blue black at maturity. Some of the varieties are 'Dentata', and 'Dentato-variegata'.

Hedera Nepalensis: Nepal Ivy

As you might expect, this species is native to Nepal and grows not only in India but throughout Southeast Asia. It was discovered by N. Wallich in 1824. In its juvenile stage it can be identified by its narrow, tapering leaves, which are a dull green color mottled with areas of gray green. There are between two and four narrow lobes on each side of the leaf, although young leaves do not always show this lobing. The hairs are scaly, more often twelve to fifteen rays and yellowish brown. The hairs are abundant on the stems, infrequent on juvenile foliage, and absent on mature leaves. The adult leaves are narrow and tapering, unlobed, and have a wavy form. The fruit is fairly large and is orange in color.

Hedera nepalensis is not hardy in northern regions of the United States and not commonly cultivated. I understand that it has been offered for sale as "Oak-leaved ivy." I do not have any in my collection, nor do my friends who grow ivy. I include it here because it does exist. If you can find this species you'll have a delightful addition to your collection. A friend of mine was in India recently and was offered plants called Nepalensis, but they turned out to be varieties of *Hedera helix* even though they produced a yellow orange fruit.

Hedera Rhombea: Japanese Ivy

This ivy species grows all over Japan except in the most northern regions. Its juvenile leaves are three-to five-lobed, and they are egg shaped. Its veins are depressed. It is graceful and has a wider range of color than most other ivies. *Hedera rhombea*'s hairs are grayish brown and scaly with seven to fourteen rays. In the adult stage the leaves are unlobed, narrow, and tapering in form. It is not reliably hardy, and so it should be grown outdoors or in a cold frame.

There is a variegated clone called 'Variegata,' which is extremely rare. Its leaves are bright green with a narrow white border around them.

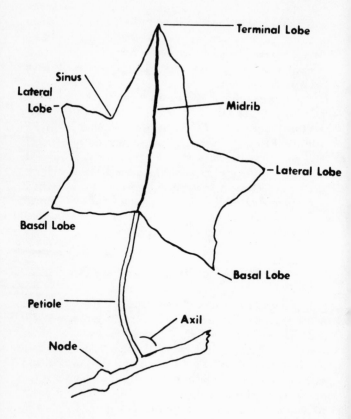

Ivy Terms Made Easy

Midrib	The rib that runs vertically from petiole to the top of the terminal lobe.
Lobe	A projection of a leaf regardless of shape.
Terminal Lobe	The projection at the top of leaf.
Lateral Lobes	The projections at the side of leaf. It is found on leaves with five lobes or more.
Basal Lobes	The projections found at base of leaf. The basal lobes are sometimes so small they go almost unnoticed.
Petiole	The supporting stalk or stem of a leaf.
Sinus	The angle or curve between two lobes.
Axil	The angle between the petiole and the vine.
Node	The joint of the vine where a petiole grows.

Bird's Foot

'PEDATA'   'STAR'
'CAENWOODIANA'   'IRISH LACE'
'SHANNON'   'PLUME D'OR'
'SHAMROCK'   'ITSY BITSY'
                'SAGITTAEFOLIA'

5.

Bird's Foot Ivies

THIS GROUP of ivy is easily identified. If you've ever seen the track of a bird's foot in sand, then you'll be quick to spot this most interesting ivy. The resemblance to a bird's foot is most obvious in the miniatures of this group, particularly in 'Irish Lace.' In all varieties, the terminal lobe on each leaf is long and thin, and the lateral lobes spread out almost making right angles.

However, within the group itself there are some puzzlements. Several named varieties are so much alike that they sometimes defy identification. 'Pedata' and 'Caenwoodiana' are good examples. The most knowledgeable ivy fanciers often find it impossible to distinguish between the two. The ivy experts from the Brooklyn Botanical Garden state that they cannot identify mature plants of comparable age of these two varieties.

Hedera Helix 'Pedata'

This outdoor-indoor climber has a dainty leaf and a tidy habit of growing that makes it marvelous for hanging baskets, in flower arrangements, on walls, and as a ground cover. Another delightful use of this Ivy is to plant it inside a kitchen window as the Victorians used to do. Some of the vines can be trained to go up and across the window frame and down the other side, which makes quite a charming sight when fully grown and one that may be enjoyed all year round.

SIZE AND SHAPE: *Hedera helix* 'Pedata' consists of leaves divided into five lobes with the middle lobe long and thin. The sinuses between the terminal and lateral lobes are very broad. Occasionally, you will find one or two slight protrusions of the sides of the terminal lobe. The basal lobes point backward like the heel of a bird's foot. Typical plants have leaves about one and one half inches long, but they vary and you may find them as small as one inch and as large as three inches.

COLOR: The leaves start life as a bright apple-green and become progressively darker as they mature until they are almost gray green. The veins are silvery and raised, accentuating the footlike appearance of the leaf.

HABIT OF GROWTH: Because it is a fast grower with a graceful vining habit, be careful where you put each plant because the long vines will quickly find their way into places they don't belong. However, 'Pedata's' fast-growing habit can be used to great advantage when you need something covered fast. Try it over a trellis or on a split-rail fence.

CULTURE: It will grow equally well in sun or shade, but the nodes will be more widely spaced if grown in the shade. Try layering this variety. Take the longest vines and attach them to the ground with a heavy wire or the hooked end of a clothes hanger. They should root quickly.

Hedera Helix
'Caenwoodiana'

The description given for 'Pedata' accurately describes 'Caenwoodiana'. However, it has less-pronounced basal lobes than 'Pedata,' and are so often undefined that you might think it had three lobes instead of five.

Hedera Helix 'Shannon'

In this short, plump cousin to 'Irish Lace' each lobe is a little broader and the leaf base a little larger. I find it fun to grow 'Shannon' in gourds. Hollow out a dried gourd and put in a few cuttings either in water or soil. (Remember, ivy rooted in water will not do well when transferred to soil.)

SIZE AND SHAPE: 'Shannon' is a five-lobed ivy with very long terminal lobes, medium-sized lateral lobes, and small basal lobes. Each lobe is broad at its base and narrows at the tip. The lobes are so deeply indented that each looks looks like a separate leaf. Unless you examine it closely you'd think there were three leaves on each petiole. This is a most unusual characteristic for ivy and is found in both 'Shannon' and 'Shamrock'. Leaves, young and old, tend to be small, with the largest about one and one half inches. Because of the deep indentation and the oddity of the lobes, the leaves have a tendency to appear much smaller than they really are.

COLOR: Young leaves are apple-green and become progressively darker as they mature. The veins are a light shade of green and are raised.

HABIT OF GROWTH: This is a vining plant, but like 'Irish Lace' it has the same ability to grow many leaves out of one node. The nodes, being closely spaced, give the plant a beautiful, bushy, full look.

CULTURES 'Shannon' is an indoor grower. Give leaves an occasional water spray and once in a while douse entire plant under the faucet. Watch out for red spider mites.

Hedera Helix
'Shamrock'

One of the prettiest topiaries I ever saw was a "poodle" made with 'Shamrock'. It looked almost real enough to bark, and it won a "first" at the International Flower Show in New York City for Mrs. Colby Chester of Greenwich, Connecticut.

'Shamrock' is unusual and a fast grower. It's not only good for topiaries, it's also good for flower arrangements and table decoration. But it's not easy to find. Contact one of the ivy growers listed in the back of the book.

SIZE AND SHAPE: The variety in the size of the leaves on this plant is astonishing. Some are tiny enough to resemble miniatures while others are an inch or two long. And they are all on the *same* vine. 'Shamrock,' like 'Green Ripple,' has a tendency to grow many leaves from one axil, which gives it a clustered look. An extra advantage is its self-branching quality. All this plus the fact that the leaves lie flat makes this ivy especially ideal for topiaries.

The leaf has five lobes, but the terminal and two lateral lobes are so equal in size that the leaf seems three-lobed. Because the sinuses are so deeply cut, each leaf appears to be three leaves clustered together. On some older leaves, the side lobes fold forward against the terminal lobe giving the leaf a layered look. It's really a great plant to study and is full of surprises.

COLOR: A rich dark green characterizes 'Shamrock'.

HABIT OF GROWTH: Its habit of growth is one of its real assets. If you want a lovely, long trailing vine, 'Shamrock' has it. If you want lots of leaves for a fuller effect, 'Shamrock' will provide you with it.

CULTURE: I find it will withstand more sunshine than most ivies. Because of its overlapping habit, a frequent thorough spraying with water will do it a world of good.

Hedera Helix
'Star'

I think you'll like this one immensely. Its habit of growth is beautiful, and its leaves look like the top half of a star. 'Star' can be used in most topiaries, but don't use it where you need sharp definition such as in an animal form. It would look marvelous on a ring, spiral, or geometric form. In the summer, grow it in an outdoor container with red, white, and blue petunias. The sight is spectacular.

SIZE AND SHAPE: Although its lobes are slender, the leaves are certainly broader than most Bird's Foot ivies. Compare it with 'Irish Lace' or 'Shannon' and you'll quickly see how much broader it is. But a Bird's Foot it is, with long lobes and deeply cut sinuses. There are five lobes on each leaf, and each is sharply pointed. The leaves vary from one inch to one and one half inches.

COLOR: 'Star' has a healthy grass-green color that is very lovely. The veins have practically the same color as the leaves, and the vines are reddish.

HABIT OF GROWTH: It is supposed to be self-branching, and it is from time to time, but I have found that if you want to have a really full plant, it should be cut back. However, the long vines are so graceful as they twist and turn to reveal their star-like leaves that you may want to let the plant grow the way it wants to.

CULTURE: 'Star' does well in partial sunshine. It is definitely not hardy. In colder regions don't try to grow it out of doors except in containers that can be brought inside in the autumn.

Hedera Helix 'Irish Lace'

My favorite by far of all the Bird's Foot ivies is 'Irish Lace'. It is the darling of the topiary fanciers and excels as an indoor plant. For a unique arrangement put a little soil into a large conch or decorative seashell and plant 'Irish Lace' in it. The effect makes quite a conversation piece.

SIZE AND SHAPE: This is the true Bird's Foot ivy. While the others remind you of a bird's foot, 'Irish Lace' *looks* like one with its delicate, long, thin five-lobed leaves. They are truly extraordinary in shape. Some of the lobes are over an inch long and only an eighth of an inch wide. Absolutely lovely.

COLOR: A rich, alive, grass-green with lighter green veins describes Irish Lace.

HABIT OF GROWTH: Though its vines grow long, they are generously leafed—sometimes with as many as five leaves growing out from a single node. This gives each long strand a full, bushy appearance. There is only one imperfection to this otherwise perfect ivy variety. Occasionally the leaf shape, which makes the plant so unique, loses its thin, spindly appearance and grows into a broader leaf resembling 'Pedata'.

CULTURE: In colder regions it must be grown indoors. It thrives on love and care, and you should spray is regularly with water.

Hedera Helix 'Plume d'Or'

This is the big brother to 'Irish Lace'. It is like 'Irish Lace' in every way except that its leaves are larger.

Hedera Helix 'Itsy Bitsy'

The 'Itsy Bitsy' is a most unusual plant and a charmer. This is the one to have on display when the ladies from the garden club visit. Not many people grow it because it isn't sold in many nurseries. I've found it at Merry Gardens in Maine and The Garden Spot in South Carolina. For those who know and love ivy, 'Itsy Bitsy' is a big favorite. Since the curve of each vine is so strongly evident, it can be used with excellent effect in "line" arrangements.

SIZE AND SHAPE: A Bird's Foot with a plus: On each petiole you'll find a leaf, but then in the larger axils you'll find a cluster of tiny leaves, some no more than a quarter of an inch long. Yet each is perfectly Bird-Foot shaped. The net effect is a beautiful, bushy ivy bursting forth with itsy bitsy leaves. The leaves are no more than an inch long and about three quarters of an inch wide from point to point of the lateral lobes.

COLOR: The larger leaves are a rich lime-green. The little quarter-inch leaves clustered between them are lemon-lime. The veins are whitish and not strongly pronounced.

HABIT OF GROWTH: 'Itsy Bitsy' is very compact and grace-ful with the entire vein curling backward forming a letter U. Interesting.

CULTURE: Look for an important spot in your plant col-lection for this one. Give it a good strong northern light and a good spraying once a week in the sink to make sure that no insects have set up housekeeping in those clusters of tiny leaves.

**Hedera Helix
'Sagittaefolia'**

This is a dainty, perfectly shaped Bird's Foot with one bad habit. For no reason at all a branch may revert to one of its ancestors, and, instead of having delicate, tiny leaves, it sprouts some that are large and clumsy looking.

SIZE AND SHAPE: This ivy has a flat leaf that is generally about an inch long. The leaf appears to be somewhat smaller, however, because the terminal lobe is so long and slender.

COLOR: 'Sagittaefolia' has an attractive, solid green leaf.

HABIT OF GROWTH: The leaves on this plant are plentiful, and, when cut back, grow in generous, heavy layers.

CULTURE: 'Sagittaefolia' enjoys the sun; it will do nicely in a west window.

See page 80 in the section on variegated ivy for a description of Hedera Helix 'Sagittaefolia Variegata'. The variegated variety is just like the all-green plant except for coloring.

Fans

'CALIFORNIA FAN'   'FAN'
'GREEN RIPPLES'   'PIXIE'
'GREEN SPEAR'

6.
The Fans

THE FAN-SHAPED ivies are unique, with very broad leaves, some of which are reminiscent of the fans carried by the Ziegfeld girls, the beauties of the Roaring Twenties, and some look like fat chubby hands. The leaves generally have five to nine lobes of equal length and are easy to identify.

The fans are all very graceful, and none of them has that coarse leathery look found in so many ivies. I give my fans a prominent position in my home because they are so different looking and certainly not the usual variety of either house plant or ivy.

Fans do very well under electric light and can be placed on coffee or end tables to garner the attention they deserve. But, of course, that means more care on your part—more watering and showering.

Hedera Helix 'California Fan'

This plant is lush enough and has such a compact habit of growth that you may be forgiven for not recognizing it as an ivy. Of all the fan-shaped ivies, this is my favorite. I am particularly fascinated by the young leaves that start life with almost no indication of a lateral or basal lobe but are rather like little fingers stretching out from a plump little palm (See page 44). Because this ivy is so compact and slow to trail, it makes a marvelous plant for a table top.

SIZE AND SHAPE: This ivy can have from five to nine lobes. (I have a plant with five-, seven-, and nine-lobed leaves *all* on the same vine.) The leaves range in size from one and one-half to two inches. Even in their fully grown state, the leaves are broader than they are long, and the lobes are short and abruptly acute. 'California Fan' reminds me a little of another fan, 'Old Garden', and it's easy to confuse one with the other.

COLOR: The young leaves have an alive apple-green appearance. The older leaves are a midsummer grass-green. The midrib is pronounced and the small veins radiating from it form a beautiful, intricate pattern. When examined closely, each leaf looks like a mosaic.

HABIT OF GROWTH: Compact and generous with leaves, 'California Fan' has a tendency to branch from the base with more than one leaf growing from each node.

Hedera Helix
'Green Ripples'

I'm including 'Green Ripples' with Fans because it fits the group. But if you study it carefully, you'll find it is also much like the Bird's Foot ivies. It can be best described as a cross between the two. Its leaves are flat like the Fans, but their long terminal lobes are much like the Bird's Foot.

SIZE AND SHAPE: The distinguishing feature of 'Green Ripples' is the size and length of the basal lobes on some of the leaves. The basal lobe is quite long, extending halfway up the leaf, which makes it look longer than it looks wide. But this occurs on only some of the leaves. Adding to the confusion is the fact that not all the leaves on the same vine are alike. Some have rounded basal lobes, giving the leaf a wide appearance.

On all leaves, however, a little pleat forms between the terminal and lateral lobes. Occasionally you'll also find a pleat between the lateral and basal lobe. These give the leaves a hint of a rippled look. The medium-size leaves grow from one inch to two and one-half inches. The majority of the leaves on my own plants seem to be longer than they are broad.

HABIT OF GROWTH: It is generous in its growth. Occasionally you'll find clusters of leaves coming from the axils. As the vine gets older it seems to lose this habit of growth, and so if you want a full bushy plant, keep it trimmed back. However, when not cut back, the leaves on the long trailing vines are very gracefully arranged and give a flowing effect.

Hedera Helix 'Fan'

It is not easy to distinguish one Fan from another. The leaves of all Fans are broader than they are long, and this is markedly true with 'Fan.'

SIZE AND SHAPE: The five to seven short, fat-lobed leaves have shallow sinuses that form a pleat or wave. The older leaves are about two inches wide and about one and one half inches from the tip of the petiole to the tip of the terminal lobe. The young leaves are about three quarters of an inch long and one inch wide.

COLOR: A very delicate pastel green describes this plant.

In most ivies the older leaves turn a darker green, but 'Fan' keeps the color of its youth. The veins are raised and very pronounced. The veins in the older leaves take on a whitish color.

HABIT OF GROWTH: A nice vining habit with the leaves staggered along the stem makes each vine look quite bushy. 'Fan' doesn't grow very fast, and so you won't have much need to cut it back. When it does get long enough, don't fail to make a cutting to plant next to the mother plant for a fuller, more bushy look. Another way to get a fuller look is to layer the ivy. See Chapter 3.

Hedera Helix 'Pixie'

This is a beautiful example of ivy showing its sense of humor. Maybe that's why this plant is called 'Pixie'. Its leaves are a cross between a Bird's Foot and a Fan. The effect is interesting and very pretty.

SIZE AND SHAPE: Over all, it is a small-leafed ivy. Some of the leaves are so small (one quarter of an inch) that they could be classified as miniatures. Others are one to one and one half inches long. The leaves have five to seven lobes. Most have two pairs of lateral lobes very sharply defined, as fan-shaped ivies are, and a long terminal lobe, but their terminal lobes are extended, thus giving a resemblance to the Bird's Foot group.

COLOR: The younger leaves have a rich, grass-green color. The older ones are a jade-green.

HABIT OF GROWTH: 'Pixie' is a slow-growing, compact plant. On some vines the leaves are clustered. On others they are densely shingled.

CULTURE: 'Pixie' can take more sun than most ivies. I've grown mine in a very sunny window, and the color has not bleached out.

Hedera Helix 'Green Spear'

'Green Spear' is a graceful plant and rather lavish with leaves.

SIZE AND SHAPE: It is shaped like a Fan except that the terminal lobe pokes out like a spear. It's a five-lobed leaf, and all lobes are sharply pointed. They are about one and one half inches long and one inch wide. The strongly indented sinuses are as sharply pointed as the tops of the lobes.

COLOR: The young leaves are lime-green and rather delicate in texture. The old leaves are dark green and leathery,

The whitish veins are more apparent on the older leaves.

HABIT OF GROWTH: The vines grow long and become very willowy and graceful. The leaves grow about one-half to three-quarter of an inch apart and are not as close to each other as they look, but because there are clusters of tiny leaves growing from the axils, which are shaped exactly like the larger leaves, the vines appear to be covered with leaves.

CULTURE: 'Green Spear' should be grown in a west window. A little sun is good for this plant.

Curlies

'TELECURL'   'PARSLEY CRESTED'
'CURLILOCKS'   'RIPPLES'
'MANDA'S CRESTED'   'IVALACE'
'FLUFFY RUFFLES'   'ABUNDANCE'

7.
The Curlies

PLEASE FORGIVE ME if I rhapsodize about curly ivies. I think they are beautiful in the way their leaves curl and overlap in delightful ripples, ruffles, and pleats. The leaf formations are so remarkably intricate, the texture so delightful to touch, and their shades of green so exquisite that to me they are the spellbinders of the ivy world.

As a group, the Curlies will take more sunshine than most ivies (except the Variegateds), but full sun tends to fade their color. Curlies need a refreshing dousing in the sink more often than most ivies because of all those ripples and ruffles in their leaves that provide a great haven for spider mites.

Hedera Helix 'Telecurl'

'Telecurl' is a beauty that originated in the 1950s. Because of its shape, I believe it to be a sport of 'Merion Beauty', which in turn is a sport of 'Pittsburgh', and therefore it is fairly hardy. 'Telecurl' looks beautiful in flower arrangements. When the arrangement loses life, make cuttings of 'Telecurl'.

SIZE AND SHAPE: Its leaves are so deeply curled that some look as though there were three leaves coming out of a single petiole. Each leaf is a ruffled beuaty unto itself with no consistent method of curling.

The number of lobes vary. On the three-lobed leaves, the lobes are more or less of equal size, whereas those leaves with five lobes have larger terminal and lateral lobes, smaller basals. Occasionally you'll find a seven-lobed leaf. Leaves vary in size from one to one and one half inches.

COLOR: The color in the younger leaves is a lovely apple-green. As the leaf grows older it becomes avocado-green. The veins are hardly discernible and are a bit paler than the leaf itself. Sinuses are deep.

HABIT OF GROWTH: It is a compact plant with a strong tendency to branch from its base. Since it's a slow grower, it will take some time filling in an area, but once it has, you'll have a rippling, wavy carpet of green.

CULTURE: You can grow this beauty outdoors south of New York, but be sure to place it where it will have some protection against winter's havoc.

Hedera Helix Cristata 'Curlilocks'

'Curlilocks' has a beautiful and probably the tightest curl of all the Curlies. As you examine individual leaves, you'll find each one quite beautiful, but because of the leathery texture of the deep-green leaves, the total effect is less graceful than that of other curly ivies.

SIZE AND SHAPE: All the leaves are five-lobed, even the new growth. Leaves are not only more tightly curled than 'Telecurl' or 'Manda's Crested', but they are considerably smaller.

COLOR: Their color is an unbouncy, deep green. Even the new shoots, although a lighter green, do not have the luster of the other Curlies. However, a very pretty feature of 'Curlilocks' is the delicate pink color of the veins, which are particularly pronounced where the leaf joins the petiole. The pink accent is more noticeable in the younger, lighter leaves. Growing tips are reddish.

HABIT OF GROWTH: 'Curlilocks' is a self-branching plant. If not given sufficient light, the branches tend to grow long and straggly and should be cut to force branching. Alfred Graf, author of the well-known *pictorial cyclopedia of exotic plants*, "Exotica," noticed one plant of 'Curlilocks' crawling happily over the parquet floor in the RCA showroom at Radio City, New York City, growing out from a little pot of earth. He said it showed "good proof" of the plant's adaptability.

CULTURE: Give it good, strong northern light.

Hedera Helix
'Manda's Crested'

Exciting! Gorgeous! There aren't enough adjectives to describe my favorite of all the curly ivies. Mrs. Otto Buettner of Stamford, Connecticut, an award-winning gardener, whose garden always has the most unusual plants, introduced me to this variety. She used it to edge a lovely winding path and also planted it in a fluffy mass in front of a perennial bed. She gave me a few cuttings several years ago. From just a handful of cuttings I was able to cover an entire area with this very handsome and productive ivy.

SIZE AND SHAPE: The three-inch leaves are five-lobed with a long terminal lobe and laterals almost at right angles to it. The basal lobes are about half the size of the laterals. In most cases all the lobes curve inward giving the leaf a smaller appearance than it really has. The overall effect is a crested, elegantly curled leaf.

COLOR: 'Manda's Crested' has light green leaves with still lighter veins, which grow upright on a reddish petiole. The new growth is a soft pea-green and has a faint soft-rose line along the margins. Occasionally one can observe a warm haze of rose over the entire leaf.

HABIT OF GROWTH: This plant has closely spaced ruffles of leaves. 'Manda's Crested' has a strong tendency to branch from the base of the plant and then tumble into waves of soft green foliage. Its leaves are usually uniform in size.

CULTURE: If given some protection from winter sun and drying winds it is hardy outdoors. It was propagated by W. A. Manda of New Jersey and is hardy like 'Merion Beauty' from which it sported.

Hedera Helix 'Fluffy Ruffles'

Its name describes this ivy perfectly. This plant is as deeply ruffled as 'Telecurl' but with a larger, more spectacular leaf. It is a truly mangnificent plant. Try growing 'Fluffy Ruffles' in a planter together with geraniums. The effect is worthwhile.

SIZE AND SHAPE: Five to seven shallow lobes on rounded leaves about two inches in diameter characterize 'Fluffy Ruffles.' Very undulating and crisply frilled, the lobes curl back to the petiole making each leaf a perfect ruffle. The sinuses are rather shallow

COLOR: Darker green than 'Manda's Crested', it's about the color of U.S. money The young leaves have an unusually delicate shade of apple-green. The raised veins verge on yellow and are very prominent.

HABIT OF GROWTH: Its long graceful veins seem to tumble from the plant. Since it is very self-branching, the effect is a riot of fluffy ruffles.

CULTURE: This is another curly ivy you can grow outdoors if you are careful where you put it. Its softly textured leaves do not like winter sun.

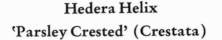

Hedera Helix
'Parsley Crested' (Crestata)

As its name suggests, there is a resemblance to the parsley leaf in this curly ivy, and it occurs on the outside edge of the leaf. Its effect is stunning, especially in a full-grown plant. It is a "must" in your collection. As a matter of fact, if I were to have only five ivies this would be one of them.

In Europe this ivy is known as 'Monstrosa', which is hardly descriptive. 'Parsley Crested' is not easy to find in your local nursery, but to track it down is well worth the effort. Check the suppliers list in the back of this book and get this beauty because it is truly lovely.

SIZE AND SHAPE: The five-lobed leaves are minutely frilled and crimped on the outside edge. The lobes are all about the same length and give the leaves a very rounded appearance. The leaves are about one and one half inches across. The frilled, fluted, ruffly, parsley-look that makes this ivy so fascinating is vaguely apparent in the young leaves. The texture of the leaves is leathery, particularly in the older leaves.

COLOR: The older leaves are parsley-green while the younger ones are apple-green, and together they make a delightful combination. The veins are quite pronounced, appearing white on the older leaves and yellowish in the younger.

HABIT OF GROWTH: 'Parsley crested' is a long-vining variety, and so I would suggest that you cut it back regularly if you want a fuller plant.

CULTURE: The more light you give this ivy, the more abundant it will be. If you are going to use it in a hanging basket or pot, put it in a partially sunny location.

Hedera Helix 'Ripples'

This is the least curly of the Curlies. It grows profusely, is unusually graceful, and always adds a bright accent wherever it is placed.

SIZE AND SHAPE: 'Ripples' is a medium-large-leafed ivy, the largest of which is about three inches wide. It has five to seven lobes, with the terminal lobe longer than the lateral. The basal lobes are not strongly pronounced. Nor is the curl of the leaf as pronounced as 'Telecurl', 'Manda's Crested', or 'Curlilocks'. The texture of the leaf not only feels delicate to the touch, but has an almost dainty appearance because of its light color.

COLOR: Both the young leaves and the older leaves have the same color—a delicate Chinese pea-pod green with the veins a shade lighter.

HABIT OF GROWTH: 'Ripples' is extravagant and graceful in its growth, with a full bushy habit of growing. The heavily loaded pendant vines have leaves that seem to shoot from every axil.

CULTURE: Some people in the Northeast (where I live) claim to have had success with 'Ripples' outdoors. I never did; but I do find it beautiful in an indoor-hanging basket. In the summer I put it in my outdoor planters.

**Hedera Helix
'Ivalace'**

The wet shine of 'Ivalace' leaves is breathtaking. The plant is a great favorite for use in topiaries because of the highly polished look of the glossy leaves. It is the smallest of all the Curlies, but its curl is minimal.

I used 'Ivalace' quite successfully on a large-size topiary shaped like a flamingo, but I was a little unhappy with the number of large leaves the plant developed. Since I tend to be a perfectionist about shape and form with my topiaries, I spent too much time picking off all the leaves that were over one inch.

SIZE AND SHAPE: Five-lobed, slightly leathery leaves with and undulating edge describe 'Ivalace.' The leaves vary in size from one half inch to one and one half inches, with the average leaf about one inch from the point where the petiole joins the leaf to the tip of the terminal lobe. The terminal lobe is sharply pronounced as are the lateral and basal lobes. The leaf has deep sinuses, and the effect is almost the shape of a maple leaf.

COLOR: The older leaves are a dark, rich, shiny green. the young leaves have a lime-green color. Veins are quite pronounced on the older leaves and are the same lime-green as the new growth. 'Ivalace' is the glossiest of all the ivies.

HABIT OF GROWTH: A self-branching, many-leaved plant, it roots quite easily but is a slow grower.

CULTURE: This is not a hardy plant in colder areas and should not be grown outdoors except in the summer. Indoors, give it plenty of light and moisture but no soggy soil. Place it in the sink once a week and give it a good spray of water, particularly on the underside of the leaves, to discourage any spider mites that might be poised for the kill.

Hedera Helix 'Abundance'

As its name implies, this beauty has an abundance of everything. The delicate curl of its vibrant green leaves, its way of spilling out of the pot, and the curve of its graceful vines make it an enchanting plant.

SIZE AND SHAPE: Most ivies grow either in a clump or they vine, and 'Abundance' does both, the result being a bushy plant with trailing vines. Because the petioles are set only one quarter of an inch apart, there is a lavish display of leaves—each vying with the other for a chance to be seen.

The leaves are broader than they are long. Depending on the light and moisture conditions under which the plant is grown, the leaves may be as large as four inches across and as small as one inch. The leaves have five to seven

lobes and get their curly look from the wavy sinuses. Lobes have a tendency to curl under.

COLOR: 'Abundance' is truly a Girl-Scout green. It's exactly the color of my daughter Elena's scout uniform. The veins are pale and tend to be yellow.

HABIT OF GROWTH: A slow, slow grower but because there is an abundance of leaves and vines this minor shortcoming should be forgiven. However, because of its slow growth you won't be able to take many cuttings.

CULTURE: For a long time I kept my 'Abundance' in a sunny south window. It was interesting to note that the leaves became lighter and smaller. For best results, put it in an east window.

Variegateds

'GOLDHEART'   'MARGINATA'
'GOLDUST'   'SUB MARGINATA'
'GLACIER'   'LITTLE DIAMOND'
'HEISE-DENMARK'   'CALIFORNIA GOLD'
          'MARMORATA ELEGANS'

8.
The Variegateds

THE COLORS of the Variegateds run from white to yellow splashed on the ivy green. They certainly add a bright note as potted plants and in arrangements.

Ivies can be variegated in many different ways, and unless you study them carefully one Variegated seems much like another. But as you study them, you'll find that some leaves are more variegated along the edges while others will be variegated white or yellow over most of the leaf. Still others will have not only lovely white and yellow patches in distinct areas but also patches of two shades of green.

Then too, as in the case of 'Tricolor', some Variegateds if grown outdoors will change color during the autumn and winter. Because the light-colored sections produce little or no chlorophyll those ivies with more green in them than variegation will root more easily than those with a larger amount of white or yellow.

A curious habit of the Variegateds (and sometimes very annoying) is their tendency to abandon their variegated pattern and become all-green leaves. I have found that the growth of the colored foliage is stimulated when insufficiently fed. I always root my variegateds in tiny two-inch pots so that when I need them in a flower arrangement I can tuck the little pots into a vase along with my flowers without having to cut my ivy.

Hedera Helix 'Goldheart'

'Goldheart' has a sunny splash of yellow on a green leaf, courtesy of Italy from which it came. It is my favorite of all the Variegateds. (See photograph on page 66.)

SIZE AND SHAPE: This is a relatively small-leafed ivy but cannot be clased as a miniature. The leaves have three to five lobes and vary from one half inch to two inches. The lobes are sharply pointed.

COLOR: Here's where 'Goldheart' is outstanding. The green on the edge is a darkly rich green. In the center there is a dollop of a rich gold-yellow. The plant looks as if the sun touched it and wouldn't go away. The yellow in 'Goldheart' is the strongest yellow found in any of the Variegateds. The stems and petioles are reddish.

HABIT OF GROWTH: Even though only one leaf comes from a node, the leaves are spaced so as to make the plant look elegantly graceful. However, it does not grow bushy and must be nudged along by cutting back regularly.

CULTURE: To help keep its gold color, place 'Goldheart' in a sunny window. The Variegateds tend to lose their brightness if not given enough sun.

Hedera Helix 'Goldust'

Take a green leaf, sprinkle it with gold dust until it has a rich mottled look, and you'll have the appearance of 'Goldust'. I first discovered 'Goldust' one spring on the top of a man-made waterfall just as dusk was falling. Surrounded by the spring green of the shrubs and trees, it looked like a huge pot of gold. It was growing in a huge flat bowl set on a rock, with the plant's graceful branches tumbling over the edges as if trying to reach the waterfall below it.

SIZE AND SHAPE: 'Goldust' has small leaves averaging no more than one inch with three to five lobes. The easiest way to identify this ivy is by its distinctive variegation.

COLOR: The Variegateds can be broadly broken down into two groups: those with an overall color pattern and those with distinct areas of color separation. 'Goldust' is in the first category with its flecks of unripened-lemon yellow and rich dark green, which often merge into a very pleasant blotched or mottled effect. The older leaves tend to lose this mottled effect although a hint of it usually remains.

HABIT OF GROWTH: 'Goldust' is a slow grower and not self-branching. If you cut it back and force it to branch you'll eventually get a marvelous, bushy plant. Don't forget to root the cuttings.

**Hedera Helix
'Glacier'**

Whenever I contemplate the Variegateds I become awed by nature's artwork. A casual glance at 'Glacier' tells you it has cream and green colors, but study it, particularly the young leaves, and you'll see what a magnificent technician nature really is. Its color and the arrangement of the color on the leaves is beautiful.

It is often difficult to distinguish the various Variegateds from each other, even when you place them side by side. Nature puts an individual touch on each one of them, sometimes so subtle you have to hunt for it. Try a half-dozen plants of 'Glacier' indoors for winter brightness. Use it as a contrasting color in your hanging baskets.

SIZE AND SHAPE: 'Glacier's' leaves are five-lobed and small. They measure from one half inch to one and one half inches and are roughly triangular. Because of the angle of the terminal lobe, the basal lobes don't appear to be very developed. The veins are raised, and the leaves are somewhat leathery to the touch.

COLOR: 'Glacier's' leaves run from light gray-green to dark gray-green and are outlined with creamy white edges. Occasionally you'll find a leaf more creamy than green. Sometimes, and particularly on the new shoots, you'll find an edge of pink. The veins are cream colored.

HABIT OF GROWTH: A reluctant rooter and a slow grower makes 'Glacier' ideal for spots where you do not want the ivy to take over. It has good vining growth. If you want to force branching, do a little pruning.

CULTURE: Use a well-drained soil and don't ever let it get water-logged. Be patient when making cuttings. Just when you think they'll never root, the roots appear. 'Glacier' can be grown outdoors all year round in areas south of New Jersey.

Hedera Helix 'Heise-Denmark'

This plant shows that it loves the sun and warm summer weather by its delightful variegation. Because of its bushy quality, 'Heise-Denmark' isn't suitable for hanging baskets, but a flat container filled with it will give you a warm, happy look all year round.

SIZE AND SHAPE: Because of its coloring this Variegated will sometimes be difficult to distinguish from 'Glacier.' However, 'Heise-Denmark's' five-lobed leaves are broader and less triangular and is also bushier. The leaves have shallower sinuses than 'Glacier', and the veins are raised.

COLOR: The shades of cream and green are almost identical to 'Glacier's.' However, grown under the conditions I grow mine—less than half a day of sunlight—the leaves are a little less creamy than those of 'Glacier's'. Its narrow creamy edge sometimes runs towards the center of the leaf,

giving an extra splash of color. In the spring, the new leaves become intensely variegated around the edges.

HABIT OF GROWTH: 'Heise-Denmark' is a better grower than 'Glacier' and tends to become bushy by itself without pruning.

CULTURE: Keep in a sunny place and spray it regularly with water. Do not overfeed.

Hedera Helix
'Marginata'

'Marginata' is one of the oldest ivies in existence. As far back as 1893, Mr. Shirley Hibbard, an Ivy expert in England, wrote a monograph on ivy and not only did he describe 'Marginata', but he listed the other different types known at that time: 'Marginata Grandis', 'Marginata Major', 'Marginata Media', 'Marginata Minor', 'Marginata Rubra'. Since the variations among these types are so negligible, they will not be described here.

The years have not been kind to 'Marginata,' and it seems to have gone out of fashion. It is difficult to buy and is grown only by a few ivy specialists. In the years since Mr. Hibbard wrote his monograph, many other Variegateds that resemble 'Marginata' have come into being, and they are not only more attractive, but they are more readily available.

The cream color of the leaf is the same color as a white poinsettia. At Christmastime, set your white poinsettia in a larger pot and then place cuttings of 'Marginata' around it for a lovely combination.

SIZE, SHAPE, AND COLOR: This plant is small and has slightly leathery, triangular-shaped leaves with three to five lobes. It is a gray-green ivy that looks as if each leaf were painted on its rich cream background. The edges of the new young leaves are reddish tinged. The veins are raised and appear grayish on the green area are only vaguely discernible on the cream area.

HABIT OF GROWTH: Many years ago in California I owned a plant of 'Marginata' so old that the base of the plant was as thick as my wrist. It grew in a large redwood planter about a yard in diameter and wove its way in and out of a lattice fence for over 200 feet.

CULTURE: This ivy is hardy and does well outdoors in areas south of New York. It will take more sunshine and neglect than most ivies.

Hedera Helix 'Sub-Marginata'

On most ivies I prefer the younger leaves. 'Sub-Marginata' is one exception; the older leaves have a thin edging of cream against a very dark black-green leaf, and the effect is startling and dramatic. The plant doesn't have a profusion of leaves, but it is graceful just the same.

If there is an abundance of the older black-green leaves on your plant, try them in an arrangement with white flowers for a dramatic effect.

SIZE AND SHAPE: Its leaves are five-lobed, but the basal lobes are so vaguely defined that it would be easy to err and call this ivy three-lobed. The leaves are much smaller than 'Marginata' and vary from one half inch to one and one half inches. The veins of the 'Sub-Marginata' are flat, and its very shallow sinuses are hardly noticeable.

COLOR: 'Sub-Marginata' is unusual in its coloring. The young leaves are gray-green with a thin cream edging, but the older leaves turn a completely different color—a dark black-green. Veins are gray-green.

HABIT OF GROWTH: It is a long trailing plant with leaves sparsely placed—about an inch between each node. Even though it needs it, this is one ivy that I do not prune to make it bushy. I like its long vining look, and I wouldn't for a moment touch those magnificent older leaves.

CULTURE: The 'Sub-Marginata' is hardy south of New York.

Hedera Helix 'Little Diamond'

'Little Diamond' is very similar to 'Marginata' except that the leaf edges are much whiter and the plant has a fuller habit of growth. Try to get 'Little Diamond' for your collection. It is a most satisfying plant.

SIZE AND SHAPE: The leaves are triangular with five lobes.
The sinuses are not very pronounced, making the leaves
appear to have only three lobes. The leaves are small—from
three quarter inch to one and one half inches long.

COLOR: Of all the Variegateds, this one seems to have the
whitest edging. It's as near a pure white as you will find
on ivy. The green in the center of the adult leaf is two-
toned—a gray-green and darker gray-green. In the young
leaves, the color is apple-green and slowly darkens to gray-
green as it matures. The veins are white and are raised.

HABIT OF GROWTH: 'Little Diamond' is a very full ivy.
The leaves seem to grow on top of each other and are
clustered so tightly that you can hardly see the vine. In
an ivy with a distinct vining habit, this tight clustering
is an unusual (and pleasant) trait.

CULTURE: This plant needs a protected spot if grown
outdoors.

Hedera Helix 'California Gold'

This plant is a mutant of Weber's California, and it is
not one of my favorites because it can't make up its mind
whether to be a Variegated or just an all-green "ivy-ivy."
I grow 'California Gold' only because I collect all varieties
of ivy.

SIZE AND SHAPE: 'California Gold' is broad leafed with
five to seven lobes that are fairly obvious. Leaves are of
uniform size, about one to two inches long. The easy way
to identify this ivy is not by its shape but by its dubious
variegation.

COLOR: Even if someone sent me a good-size cutting of
'California Gold', it would be quite possible to make a
mistake in identification. That's because its leaves start out

life completely green and quite ordinary looking. As the plant matures, it sends out a shoot with mottled creamy yellow and green leaves. This variegation is not particularly interesting or pretty. Because many of the leaves on the plant are all green, the variegated ones appear to have an iron deficiency rather than a variegated look.

HABIT OF GROWTH: What it lacks in variegation it makes up in form. It's self-branching, and you don't have to lift a knife to get it this way. It is a slow grower.

CULTURE: This ivy does best in a window or room that gets partial sunshine.

Hedera Helix 'Marmorata Elegans'

There are three other ivies so similar to 'Marmorata elegans' that I have often wondered why they were given the separate names of 'discolor', 'dealbata', 'Howardi'. The description below for 'Marmorata elegans' fits all three.

SIZE AND SHAPE: 'Marmorata elegans' is a robust, old-time variety with triangular-shaped leaves and mostly with five lobes. Adult leaves are about one and one half inches to two inches long and about the same width at the broadest part.

COLOR: The color, particularly in the summer time, is

an unusually bright mottled green. The all-over effect of mottling makes it difficult to tell whether it is green splashed with white or white splashed with green.

In winter the leaves show very little mottling. Even their shade of green that looks so vibrant in the summer is quite different. One would think you were growing two plants. But it does make for an interesting and unusual effect.

CULTURE: A winter hardy ivy as far north as New York City, 'Marmorata elegans' will do well in partial sun.

Hedera Helix 'Sagittaefolia Variegata'

This delightful beauty is a variegated Bird's Foot. It has all the good color qualities of the Variegateds as well as the delicately shaped form of the Bird's Foot ivies.

SIZE AND SHAPE: 'Sagittaefolia' is a flat growing Bird's Foot leaf, but it looks as if the bird had flat feet. Since each leaf is very flat and grows in the same direction from its petiole, the entire vine takes on a "just ironed" look.

This habit of growth is quite unique for ivy and gives the plant a neat, crisp, almost starched look.

The leaves are generally an inch long, but because the terminal lobe is so long and slender, they appear to be smaller than they really are.

COLOR: Strongly variegated. Generally creamy white around the edges with two shades of gray-green in the center. Occasionally the gray-green has a speckled look. The green of the new growth is almost apple green. The veins are whitish and look particularly pretty when seen against the gray-green.

HABIT OF GROWTH: The vines are heavily leafed. If you cut them back, the new growth will shoot out a profusion of leaves causing the vine to be laded down with a layered cluster of leaves. Really beautiful.

CULTURE: Keep in a west window. It likes a little sun.

Heart Shapes

'SCUTIFOLIA' (CORDATA)   'MY HEART'
'SWEETHEART'   '238TH STREET'
'GLYMII'

9.
The Heart Shapes

SOME IVY fanciers have nicknamed this ivy class, "the Valentines." Heart shaped they certainly are and very easy to identify. The varieties in this group are all very similar with true heart-shaped leaves, and they differ mainly in the size of their leaf.

They all have a very dark leathery look and are rarely lobed. The prettiest of the group in my estimation is 'Sweetheart'. 'Sweetheart' not only grows more leaves on each vine, but the leaves grow closer together than other Heart Shapes, which gives it a full, bushy, really lush look. All the ivies in the group look beautiful as table decorations for bridal showers and valentine parties.

One idiosyncrasy should be mentioned here. The majority of outdoor ivies when they reach their adult stage (when they stop climbing) tend to lose their sinuses and take on a heart shape. Don't be misled if you see heart-shaped ivy growing outdoors and call it a true Heart Shape when its juvenile plant is a member of an entirely different group. (See Chapter 12.)

An exception to this is 'Glymii' and an uncommonly hardy outdoor ivy called '238th Street' (because that is the street in New York City where it was found). It belongs to the heart-shaped group because its juvenile as well as its adult foliage is heart shaped.

Hedera Helix 'Scutifolia' (Cordata)

Mrs. Carolyn Koch (of International Geranium Society fame), who collects everything heart shaped from Christmas tree ornaments to desert plates, gave me a 'Scutifolia' over ten years ago. Maybe I like it more than it deserves because of my warm friendship with Mrs. Koch, but being a realistic soul, I cannot class it as one of the prettier ivies, despite its lovely heart-shaped leaves. (See page 82).

SIZE AND COLOR: The leaves are so perfectly heart shaped that the sinuses barely exist. Leaves vary from one inch to one and one half inches.

COLOR: 'Scutifolia's' color is a rich, deep matte green with pale veining.

HABIT OF GROWTH: Because the leaves are widely separated (about an inch apart), the overall effect is sparse and not graceful. There is no lively tumbling appearance, which is found in so many other ivies. If you don't want it to become long and straggly, cut it back regularly and the plant will take on a more compact appearance.

CULTURE: Given too much sun, the leaves of this plant will take on a darker hue. To keep your leaves viable, find a spot with northern exposure.

Hedera Helix 'Sweetheart'

My favorite of the Heart Shapes. It has beautifully shaped leaves, and a lot of them for a heart-shaped ivy. Its neat habit of growth and cheerful green color make it a delight. Normally, I don't like to use a leaf-shine spray. However, the leaves on 'Sweetheart' are so perfectly heart shaped that you may want to show them off. Wash them spotlessly clean and then spray them with leaf shine.

SIZE AND SHAPE: 'Sweetheart' is the smallest of the group. The leaves are from one half to one inch long and wide, and they rarely lose their heart shape. My 'Sweetheart' is quite old, and in the considerable length of time I have had it, not one leaf has varied from its heart shape.

COLOR: A bright jade green describes the color of this heart-shaped ivy.

CULTURE: It's a pleasure to give this one loving care although it doesn't require much attention. Partial sun, moist soil with good drainage, and a weekly dousing are all that 'Sweethearts' need.

Hedera Helix 'My Heart'

This ivy is the largest of the Heart Shapes, but it is too long, straggly, and sparse for my taste.

SIZE AND SHAPE: The leaves are usually true heart shaped, but occasionally you'll find a maverick that hints of a lobe. The medium-large leaves (two and one half to three inches) are sturdy and leathery. Even the petioles, which are normally so delicate, are not only long but thick and feel more like a vine than a petiole.

COLOR: 'My Heart' is a very dark black-green and is slightly waxy in appearance. The light veins contrast sharply with the leaf. The petioles and vines are a brownish red.

HABIT OF GROWTH: This plant is not self-branching and will look like a long stringy vine if you don't cut it back.

CULTURE: 'My Heart' will stand more sun than most ivies, but the leaves will look more delicate (and prettier) if not grown in full sun. This Heart Shape does well in northerly light.

Hedera Helix
'Glymii'

If you want to grow an outdoor ivy that doesn't look like most, then try this one. Its heart-shaped leaves make it an unusual ivy, but because the leaves are small and the distance between each leaf is wide, the total effect is skimpy. If you want a really lush, heart-shaped outdoor ivy use '238th Street'.

SIZE AND SHAPE: 'Glymii's' leaves are small—about one inch long—and most definitely shaped like a heart. Technically it is a three-lobed leaf, but many of the leaves show no indentation of the sinuses and you may not be aware of the individual lobes. However, the leaves vary on the vine, and some have a slight indentation that distorts the heart shape. The new leaves are cupped but tend to flatten out as they get older.

COLOR: This plant has a dark leathery leaf with wiry green vines.

HABIT OF GROWTH: This Heart Shape is a good creeper, hugging the surface with its aerial rootlets. It will grow indoors, but the sparseness of the leaves on the vine does not make it a particularly appealing indoor plant.

CULTURE: 'Glymii' should be grown outdoors in a protected location. Because of the profusion of its aerial rootlets it does well against buildings, trellises, and is marvelous for layering. Just put a stone on top of the vine to hold it down. In a short time it will have attached itself to the ground, forming a new plant.

Hedera Helix '238th Street'

Here's a very satisfying and hardy outdoor ivy that is definitely heart shaped. It is a slow starter, but once it gets going, watch out. It becomes so thick that it literally becomes another wall.

Mr. T. H. Everett, the former Director of Horticulture and Curator of Education for the New York Botanical Garden, came upon this heart-shaped ivy in 1935 growing in the garden of the Church of the Good Shepherd at Matilda Avenue and 238th Street in the Bronx, New York. He named it after the street on which he found it.

SIZE AND SHAPE: Most of the leaves are one and one half inches long and wide without even a hint of a sinus. The terminal lobe tends to be delicately pointed. In their adult or arborescent stage, the leaves retain their heart shape. It is one of the few ivies that easily reaches an adult or arborescent stage in a cold climate.

COLOR: Older leaves are leathery and almost a black green. The younger leaves are lighter and soft green. All the leaves have pronounced yellow veins.

HABIT OF GROWTH: This plant is a strong vigorous grower

with the petioles spaced about an inch apart. Vines are stiff. Rootlets are in abundance on each vine. A characteristic of '238th Street' is that it produces trailing vining shoots directly from mature flowering and fruiting branches. When planting this ivy, you should be sure it is planted very close to the wall so that the roots will have a chance to get a firm hold. Otherwise, when the plant becomes older and heavier, it may pull away from the wall on account of its weight.

CULTURE: This is such a strong grower that you can plant it almost anywhere—even in very cold areas—and it will do well.

Ivy-Ivies

'MERION BEAUTY'	'BUNCH'
'MAPLE QUEEN'	'WOODSII'
'GARLAND'	

10.

The Ivy-Ivies

THE OTHER chapters have dealt with ivies that are Curlies, Heart Shapes, Fans, Bird's Feet, Variegateds; and for the most part these are fairly easy to identify because they are unusual.

The plants in the group I call the Ivy-Ivies are the hardest of all to distinguish from each other because they are so similar—they look like everyone's idea of what ivy should look like. Almost all of them have pronounced terminal, basal, and lateral lobes. All have indented sinuses, and all resemble the *Hedera helix* or so-called English Ivy that most Americans think of when they think of ivy. The English, however, don't call *Hedera helix* "English." They call it "common" ivy.

Most of the ivies in this group will live outdoors in states south of New Jersey when planted in a protected spot out of the strong clear winter sun. A good rule to remember is that the ivies you plant outdoors will more likely be hurt more by winter sun than by cold frosty air.

Hedera Helix 'Merion Beauty'

If you find an ivy at your florist bursting with gay, green leaves, tumbling over in wild profusion as if trying to be the center of attention in the presence of some

91

mighty fancy competition, it's probably 'Merion Beauty' —the darling of the florist trade. It's not an unusual plant, but its bouncy way of growing, its generosity of leaves, and its fresh color make it a very satisfactory plant.

SIZE AND SHAPE: The plant runs the gamut from medium large—two and one half inches—to small, one inch five-lobed leaves. The sinuses are deeply indented, and the terminal lobe is slightly elongated.

COLOR: 'Merion Beauty' is a fresh grass-green. It is the texture of the leaf that gives the plant its healthy, fresh, just-born look. (See photograph on page 90.)

HABIT OF GROWTH: The leaves grow in great abundance on a somewhat fragile vine. The effect is a cascade of greenery tumbling all over the place. Of course, if you want a more compact plant just cut the vines—if you have the heart to.

CULTURE: Keep 'Merion Beauty' well watered, but don't let it get wet feet by allowing water to stand in the saucer.

Hedera Helix 'Maple Queen'

This is an ivy that you may find at your supermarket. In Westchester, New York, where I now live, I find it regularly at the various markets. Sometimes it is properly labeled, but most of the time marked just plain "Ivy." This annoys me considerably. Although not incorrect, such nondescriptive labeling is not dissimilar to brussel sprouts being labeled "cabbage." With a little effort the grower ought to be able to include the plant's full name.

'Maple Queen' will do very well in an office and will get you out of that philodendron syndrome. It's an easy grower, and it always looks lush and will give its owner a "green thumb" reputation.

SIZE AND SHAPE: 'Maple Queen' has medium-size leathery leaves that run from two to three and one half inches, and they look like ivy . . . most people's idea of ivy. Although the leaves are spread about one inch apart, the vine has quite a full look due to the size and overlapping of the leaves. As the leaves grow older, the veins become more pronounced. The originator and patent holder of the plant, Mr. Sylvan Hahn, evidently thought that the leaves resembled those of a maple tree, but I find this is not quite the case because of the width of the terminal lobe and the irregular size of the basal lobe.

COLOR: The leaves are waxy, rich dark green with whitish veins.

CULTURE: This ivy can be grown outdoors as far north as New York City. Since it is a sport of the 'Pittsburgh'

variety, it is a reasonably hardy plant outdoors and a good plant to use where space is limited because it does not "take over."

HABIT OF GROWTH: The vines of 'Maple Queen' grow long and need to be cut if you wish to induce branching. I do not cut mine back because the vines are so heavily covered with leaves there is never a scraggly look.

If you are looking for an ivy to take over an area, use Irish or Baltic Ivy (see chapter on Hardy Outdoor Ivy). Indoors, 'Maple Queen' does marvelously well with northern light. Give it a shower often to help it keep its clean, refreshing look.

Hedera Helix 'Bunch'

Its name describes it perfectly. No trailing vine this. It's a quiet, unpretentious, undemanding plant that you'll never have to cut back.

SIZE AND SHAPE: This ivy has a five-lobed leaf with deep sinuses. Some leaves are so decidedly lobed they remind you of a maple leaf. The leaves are about two and a half inches across and two inches long.

COLOR: The leathery textured leaves are a rich deep green.

HABIT OF GROWTH: You can't mistake this ivy: It grows in a bunch. Plant a clump in your rock garden and look at it a year later and it will still be a little bunch. It is a slow grower, as slow a grower as you'll find in ivy.

CULTURE: For this ivy, choose a moist spot that is protected from drying winds and bright winter sun. Don't grow it outdoors farther north than New York City.

Hedera Helix 'Woodsii'

'Woodsii' is a sturdy vining plant that is quite pretty in a quiet, unobtrusive manner. It looks attractive in a bowl with bright flowers. I grow my 'Woodsii' hanging from the kitchen ceiling in front of the window. It trails down the side of the wall and is now beginning to curl around my sink. My family jokes about my jungle sink, but it's the best way I know to keep a constant and admiring eye on one of my green friends.

SIZE AND SHAPE: Most of the leaves have five to seven lobes, with the basal and lateral lobes about equal in length. As you look at a leaf it seems unusually flat and therein lies its charm. Even the veins, which have a sharply contrasting color, are flat.

COLOR: 'Woodsii' is a velvety green with light yellow veins. The new leaves are apple-green.

CULTURE: You can grow this one outdoors as far north as New York City. Indoors, however, give it more sunshine than you would give the not-as-hardy types.

Hedera Helix 'Garland'

If this plant had been around in Bacchus's day, his followers would have selected it for the wreath on his head. The leaves truly do form a garland on their vine. On my Thanksgiving table, I have used 'Garland' coming out of a cornucopia accented with pomegranates and persimmons. Very decorative.

SIZE AND SHAPE: 'Garland' is a compact, bushy variety with several petioles with leaves growing from the axil. The medium-large leaves, two and one half inches to three inches, are mostly deeply lobed. Some have very pronounced lobes with deep wavy sinuses while others show very little indentation. The veins stand out sharply and give the plant a heavily textured look.

COLOR: This ivy is an apple-green with veins about the same color.

CULTURE: Find a spot in your home with northerly light. You're taking a chance if you try to grow 'Garland' outdoors in colder areas—it's a stay-at-home.

Miniatures

'TRILOBA'   'MINIMA'

'SPINOZIA'   'WALTHAMENSIS'

'JUBILEE'

II.

Miniatures

MOST OF the ivies in this group are true miniatures. That is, they are plants shaped in every way like larger-leafed ivy except that the leaves are considerably smaller—not more than one half inch in length. I have arbitrarily also included in this group two other forms of growth that to me are entitled to be called "miniature." They are

1. Plants on which you will find leaves as large as an inch or more in length but with the majority of the leaves under half an inch.
2. Plants on which the majority of leaves are about an inch, but because they are so delicate, slender, and finely cut, they appear to be miniature.

Miniatures are ideal plants for people living in small apartments. There is not only much joy in growing them, but they also take up so little space that they can even be grouped under a glass bell or a Lucite cake dome like a miniature greenhouse.

Miniatures can give a spectacular effect if used on topiaries, provided, however, that you have lots and lots of patience or lots and lots of cuttings because they are very slow growers. Many topiary experts don't use the true miniatures for this reason. Instead, they use the ones that appear to be miniatures (the number 2 group) because they grow faster.

Hedera Helix 'Triloba'

This is a miniature ivy shaped like the Ivy-Ivies. 'Triloba' is shaped in every way like its larger relatives except that it is scaled down to Tom Thumb size. I planted one of mine in a small seashell, which I keep on a carved Chinese curio shelf. Its richly black-green color gives a dramatic contrast to the mutton-fat jade perfume bottles on the shelf.

SIZE AND SHAPE: Because of the longer length of the terminal lobe, the leaves appear to be tri-lobed, thus its name 'Triloba'. However, the leaves actually have *five* distinct lobes, and the plant's name is a misnomer. Unlike 'Spinozia' and 'Jubilee', it is definitely a vining plant with leaves that are widely spaced—about three quarters of an inch to one inch apart. The smallest of the leaves are no more than one quarter of an inch long and wide. Occasionally, you'll find a leaf an inch long and wide, but most of the leaves average about one half inch.

COLOR: 'Triloba' is robust and very lush black-green with sharply contrasting whitish veins.

HABIT OF GROWTH: Because of its vining habit of growth, you will be able to take more cuttings from 'Triloba' than from most other Miniatures. Although the leaves are widely spaced on the vine, they are placed in such an orderly fashion that the effect is one of grace rather than sparseness. (See photograph on page 98.)

CULTURE: Give it good light and wash its leaves regularly. Its rich color can be enhanced with Leaf Shine. If you plant 'Triloba' in a seashell, after watering be sure to drain the shell by turning it over.

Hedera Helix 'Spinozia'

Only the expert would recognize this plant as an ivy. Planted in a dish garden, it looks like a bonzai shrub. It's a hard one to find, and few greenhouses have it.

SIZE AND SHAPE: The smallest of the leaves are no longer than one quarter inch long and one eighth inch wide. Most of the leaves are about one half inch long and one quarter inch wide. Yet there are some that are three quarters of an inch long and wide. Because of the bushy way this ivy grows, the larger leaves do not detract from the miniature appearance of the plant.

The smallest of the leaves show no indication of any terminal, lateral, or basal lobes. They are oval. It is only in the larger leaves that you are able to identify 'Spinozia' as an ivy. The larger leaves resemble the fan-shaped ivy with three quarter inch terminal and lateral lobes and clearly defined sinuses.

COLOR: The glossy leaves are a vibrant mint green. Since the color is the same on both the young and older leaves, the entire plant always looks healthy and vigorous. The veins are a lighter green. On some of the leaves the veins are so indented that they make the leaves look slightly puckered.

HABIT OF GROWTH: 'Spinozia' is densely leafed with upright, knobby vines. Some of the vines have leaves that grow close to the soil while others don't begin to leaf until the vines are three or four inches long.

CULTURE: Grow 'Spinozia' in a strong northern light, and shower the leaves regularly. If you grow it in a dish garden, be very sparing with water because dish gardens have no drainage and ivies do not like soggy soil.

Hedera Helix 'Minima'

'Minima' is a collector's ivy that is nice to have because it is an old ivy. However, you may not want to use it as a decorative house plant because it is rather straggly.

In 1893, Mr. S. Hibbard in his book on ivy called 'Minima' the "smallest-leaved ivy." It certainly is not that today.

SIZE AND SHAPE: The slightly undulating leaves are scaled down versions of the type you find on many Ivy-Ivies. They are about three quarter inch in length and width, are five-lobed, thin and leathery, and grow sparsely on the plant. The petioles are widely separated—about one and one half inches apart.

COLOR: 'Minima' is a dull dark green with gray veins and petioles.

HABIT OF GROWTH: This plant is a stingy grower that has long straggly vines unless you cut them back.

CULTURE: 'Minima' is better as an outdoor plant than it is as an indoor one. It will withstand winter temperatures as far north as New York City.

Hedera Helix 'Walthamensis'

'Walthamensis' is a small version of English Ivy. In fact, some people call it "Baby English." It is reminiscent of 'Minima,' but it is prettier with more and better shaped leaves and a jollier shade of green.

SIZE AND SHAPE: An easy way to identify this plant is to look for the sharply indented sinuses on all five lobes. Often the basal lobes on ivy leaves are so small that to find them you have to examine a leaf minutely. But on this ivy the basal lobes are clearly defined because of the depth of the sinuses. Their depth gives the leaves a slightly scalloped look. The leaves are from three quarter inch to one and one half inches long and wide.

COLOR: The new growth is a very lively shade of grass-green and tends to darken as it matures. Veins are whitish.

HABIT OF GROWTH: 'Walthamensis' is a vining plant with no self-branching habit. Its vines are slender and flexible. Although the petioles are widely spaced, the plant, because of its larger leaves, does not look as straggly as 'Minima'.

CULTURE: This is a good plant for outdoor growth in places where there are narrow areas to cover because it does not "take over," as many ivies do. This plant needs good drainage.

Hedera Helix 'Jubilee'

This miniature is by far my favorite, and it's quite likely to be yours too. It's got everything. Tiny. Colorful. Compact growth. It's even self-branching. Each little snub-nosed leaf (of which there is a profusion) is a sparkling beauty. 'Jubilee' is a must in your collection.

SIZE AND SHAPE: The smallest leaves are no more than one half inch long and wide. The largest leaves are no more than three quarter inch long and one half inch wide. The leaves are irregularly shaped, but most have three to five lobes.

It is almost impossible to describe the leaf shape because there are so many different shapes on each vine. On some, the terminal lobe is long with no hint of sinuses, which makes the leaf look like a teardrop. On others, the lateral lobes are clearly defined, and those leaves look like Ivy-Ivies. Then, there are others that have a large lateral lobe on one side only; and some have two lateral lobes that are differently shaped. Despite this marvelous variety, 'Jubilee' is an easy ivy to identify because of its very tiny leaves and variegation.

COLOR: Its three colors vie with its shape for beauty. The light silvery-green leaves are edged creamy-white with dollops of dark-green splashed on the leaves. No two leaves are colored the same. Even the veins are capricious. On some, they are hardly noticeable. On others they are raised and whitish.

HABIT OF GROWTH: 'Jubilee' is a slow, slow grower but is freely self-branching with a profusion of leaves on every vine. The leaves grow from the base of the plant, giving it a very bushy look even in a young plant.

CULTURE: It's a sturdy plant that does not need to be pampered, but because it is so pretty and such a joy to handle, I find myself following ivy-culture rules to the letter and treating 'Jubilee' like a fragile baby, which it is not. Give it plenty of humidity, not too much food, some sun, or at least good strong light.

Outdoor

ENGLISH IVY   BALTIC IVY

IRISH IVY   'PITTSBURGH'

'238TH STREET'

12.
Hardy Outdoor Ivy

HARDY outdoor ivy is not only a creator of perennial beauty but a camouflage artist and sleight-of-hand magician, too. It can be used to cover something unsightly, such as the area around your trash cans, or to cover something pretty to make it even prettier, such as a sundial. You can use it to make an area green all year long (under trees where grass won't grow). You can use it in outdoor window boxes; as a perennial green edging around flower beds; as a low hedge between houses; in the rock garden; to replace a grass lawn on a slope. It can even give your home instant age.

You can use it to cover a pole or a fence. You can train it along wires to grow as a swag or garland (see page 117). You can use it on topiary trees at your front door (see page 136). You can use it to clothe a chain link and a picket or rail fence in lush green.

One additional advantage to growing hardy outdoor ivy as a wall cover is that it is able to absorb moisture through its rootlets, which attach themselves to the wall. This will reduce dampness and will give you a drier wall.

Deciding *where* to use hardy outdoor ivy is easy compared to the experience you might encounter at your nursery when you go to *buy* it. Many nurserymen and women are most knowledgeable about everything they sell but ivy, and your conversation with one of them might go like this:

Q. What kind of outdoor ivy do you have?
A. English.
Q. Yes, but what kind?
A. It's all English. If you want to get fancy, lady, its name is *Hedera helix.*

Most ivy you see sold in garden centers *is Hedera helix*, although there are five different classes of *Hederas* and *helix* is only one (see chapter 4). There are over 100 varieties of *Hedera helix*, most of which are not hardy except in the southern part of the United States.

There is a way to tell the difference between the varieties of hardy outdoor ivy most generally sold by your local garden center. (I'm not talking about the nurseries that specialize in ivy, just the average store on the corner.) The *Hedera helix* without variety description is usually called "English." However, what most people call "English" is actually Irish Ivy (*Hedera helix* Hibernica). Here's the difference:

Hedera Helix—English Ivy

English Ivy has a rather square look and is about two and one half inches in each direction. The leaves are slightly cupped and have creamy veins. (See photograph on page 108.)

Hedera Helix Hibernica

Irish Ivy is the largest of the *helix* varieties and is a stronger, thicker growing ivy with large roundish leaves about five inches long and wide. It is the fastest growing of all the hardy outdoor ivies.

Hedera Helix Baltica

Baltic Ivy is similar to English Ivy but has smaller leaves and very pronounced white veins. Of all the hardy outdoor ivies, baltic ivy is the hardiest ivy throughout the United States and Canada.

Hedera Helix 'Pittsburgh'

'Pittsburgh' Ivy is also smaller than English Ivy and has a pronounced terminal lobe. Its veins are whiter than English but not as white as baltic.

Hedera Helix '238th Street'

'238th Street' Ivy has only three lobes and is heart shaped. (All the other hardy outdoor ivies have five lobes.) '238th Street' is also the one most inclined to produce flowers and fruit (see page 88).

All outdoor ivies go through two distinct phases—the juvenile state and the mature stage, which is called aborescence. However, with the exception of '238th Street', you will never see ivy in its arborescent stage while it is climbing and vining. Those who live in the northern regions rarely see it even on older plants. That's because arborescence does not take place until the ivy has reached a point where it has no further support to continue its climb. When that happens, it sends out horizontal branches with unlobed leaves. This is followed by clusters of rather insignificant flowers and then berries.

The curious thing is that if you live in the northern regions and train some ivy on a five-foot pole, it will eventually pass into its mature or arborescent stage when it no longer has anything to climb on. The same thing would happen if you planted the ivy at the base of a taller pole. No matter what the height of its support, ivy does not become arborescent until it has nothing more to climb or lean on. Ivy seems to know when it has no further support and drops its vining and climbing habit and becomes shrublike.

Outside the *Hedera helix* group there is an ivy that is also reliably hardy during winter throughout America. It is *Hedera colchica*. Two varieties are *Hedera colchica* dentata and *Hedera colchica* 'Dentato-Variegata'.

Hedera colchica dentata has very large leathery three-to-five-lobed leaves that grow as large as seven by ten inches. The leaves are heart shaped and quite spectacular because of their size. It should only be planted where its giant leaves won't overpower the object on which they are growing. This ivy is best not grown on homes but rather on large walls or fences. (See top of page 114.)

Hedera Colchica 'Dentato-Variegata' is a smaller version of dentata and is variegated with a bright, creamy white edge. (See photograph below.)

For culture of hardy outdoor ivy see pages 13–21.

Where To Plant

When growing up a wall, hardy outdoor ivy should be set as close as possible to the wall. If there are overhead eaves, be sure the ivy is watered regularly. Hardy outdoor ivy will stand any amount of frost provided it is not given a southern exposure. Ivy does not die in winter because of the cold. The real problem is the winter sun and drying winds. For this reason it isn't wise to plant ivy in a sunny, southern location but rather give it an eastern or northern exposure. I have friends who have broken this rule and have had excellent luck. Maybe you will, too.

When To Cut Back

When growing ivy on houses or walls, you should clip it annually, preferably in early June. This accomplishes two things. You get rid of the winter dirt and give the plant time to make new foliage before winter. If the plant is not pruned regularly it will become barren at the base and heavy with growth at the top.

For an ivy hedge, use your hedge cutter to shear. Prevent it from becoming thick and bulky by cutting out the long straggly vines with hand clippers instead of shearing them.

If your Ivy becomes too dense, sparrows will take up residence in it. Unless you're an early riser, or you love sparrows chirping at dawn, clip, clip, clip.

How To Edge a Flower Bed

Plant your ivy around the bed by pegging down the long trailing vines to form the outer edge. As it grows, shear it each spring just before the new growth starts and tuck in or snip back any wild shoots that make their appearance during the growing season.

Ground Cover

Ivy as a ground cover will thrive in either sun or shade and in all kinds of soil. However, in the drier locations and in poor soil, it will grow more slowly and bear smaller leaves. The smaller-leafed ivies make beautiful ground cover for the spring flowering bulbs.

How To Make an Ivy Hedge

For a low ivy hedge, posts should be set about six feet apart and connected with a horizontal rail set about one or two feet above the ground. Plants should be grown at each post and the growth trained onto the connecting rails. As the vines grow, fasten them to the rails until you have a thick growth. Shear for thicker growth and shape.

How To Make a Swag or Garland

Here are two ways to make a garland, and both turn out beautifully. One is to use eye hooks screwed into the wall about every three feet. Through each, loop a very strong wire and curve it into the garland shape you want. Start at both ends and train it to grow along the curve of the wire. When it gets thick, clip so that the ivy is narrower at the eye hooks than it is in the middle of the swag. (See photograph on opposite page.)

The other way is to make the garland a free-standing

unit by imbedding posts into the ground about four feet apart. Then drape a chain in a scalloped form from post to post, securing the chain with a nail or hook. Plant ivy at the end posts and train along chain.

(*Photo by Max Eckert.*)

Oddities

'BIG DEAL'	'FLEUR DE LIS'
'SMALL DEAL'	'BUTTERCUP'
'MEAGHERI'	'ERECTA'
'GREEN FEATHER'	'CONGLOMERATA'

13.
The Oddities

THE IVIES I have categorized as "Oddities" are in that
group because they simply do not fit into any other
category. They do not look like ivy, and a novice would
have difficulty identifying them as ivy. They are unusually
showy, decorative, and difficult to find. Each one is in
a class by itself and has no similarity to any other generic
group.

Hedera Helix 'Big Deal'

This is an oddball ivy. It doesn't seem to belong to the
ivy family—the spinach family, yes, and maybe a slight tie
to the geranium family. While I like spinach and have
had a lifetime love affair with geraniums, I just can't find
any affection for this ivy. But don't let my likes and
dislikes influence you. (See photograph on opposite page.)

If you want to have some fun at the garden club, take a
leaf of 'Big Deal' with you and see if the experts can
guess what plant it comes from. I did that once, and the
answers were amazing. No one guessed ivy.

SIZE AND SHAPE: Its leaves are two inches in diameter,
and to me they look as if they were under attack by an
army of leaf rollers. Years ago when I got my first plant

119

I isolated it from the rest of my ivies and sprayed it every three days with Malathion. It wasn't until a month had gone by—when the new shoots appeared and they curled under in the same fashion as the older ones—that I realized this was 'Big Deal's' normal appearance.

Because of the very rounded leaves, the lobes and sinuses are not apparent. Veins are raised and pronounced. 'Big Deal' not only looks like spinach, but it is the color of spinach. The young leaves are very shiny but tend to darken with age. The stems are reddish.

HABIT OF GROWTH: 'Big Deal' is a slow grower.

CULTURE: This plant is best suited for a southern window.

Hedera Helix 'Small Deal'

This plant is another spinach-looking-puckered ivy.

SIZE AND SHAPE: As its name suggests, 'Small Deal' is quite similar to 'Big Deal'. It has the same puckered look but not as pronounced. The big difference is in the shape of the leaves. They are slightly rounded, but at least you can see the lobes. Some of the leaves have five, seven, or nine lobes. The leaves tend to curl up and over rather than under as in 'Big Deal'. The veins are pronounced, the texture is very leathery, and the leaves feel as if they would crack to the touch.

COLOR: Like 'Big Deal', the color of this plant is a rich spinach-green with hardly any difference in color between the young and older leaves.

HABIT OF GROWTH: 'Small Deal' is a slow grower.

CULTURE: Give 'Small Deal' plenty of moisture and a spot in a southern window.

Hedera Helix 'Meagheri'

There's nothing like a good botanical controversy between friends. For years I have challenged ivy "experts" for their cavalier manner of lumping 'Meagheri' and 'Green Feather' together. While they strongly resemble each other, I do not consider them to be identical. I enjoy a good fight, and the herbal verbals that have been heaped upon me because I have dared to question the other "experts" judgment (and eyesight) only strengthens my contention. Alfred Graf's *Exotica*, a pictorial cyclopedia of exotic plants, claims that 'Meagheri' and 'Green Feather' are one and the same.

'Meagheri' was sported in the greenhouses of Fred Danker of Albany, New York, and he named it after one of his employees. Alfred Bates, a renowned horticulturist and

ivy fancier, tells in a series of articles he wrote for the National Horticulture magazine in 1940 how 'Meagheri' became 'Green Feather.' After he received a plant of 'Meagheri' from Mr. Danker, Mr. Bates remarked to a friend that it looked like a green feather. The friend suggested that he name it that. He wrote Danker who did not acknowledge his letter, but Bates called it 'Green Feather' anyway.

In my collection I have two separate and distinct plants. One is 'Meagheri' and the other 'Green Feather'. The leaves of the latter are certainly larger than the other.

SIZE AND SHAPE: The five-lobed, leathery leaves are tiny and not more than one half inch in length. They are tightly clustered, and each has a very long terminal lobe with narrow lateral lobes. The tiny basal lobes are hardly discernible.

COLOR: 'Meagheri' is a deep holly-green with the new growth a shade lighter and the veins lighter still.

HABIT OF GROWTH: It certainly takes its own sweet time branching. However, many petioles often form from one axil, which gives the plant its marvelously full look.

CULTURE: Grow 'Meagheri' in a protected location in areas south of New Jersey. It is beautiful in a rock garden where a slow growing variety is wanted. Watch out if you grow it as a pot plant. It's a haven for insects, such as the red spider, because of its closely set leaves.

Hedera Helix 'Green Feather'

This is the plant that is so often confused with 'Meagheri.' Many growers will tell you that it is the same plant. Not I.

My 'Green Feather' plant came from Mary Ellen Ross of the Merry Gardens in Camden, Maine, and a beauty it is. It is far more decorative and graceful than 'Meagheri,' and it is at the moment growing with its branches outstretched to the heavens, as if pleading, "I want to be me, not 'Meagheri'."

SIZE AND SHAPE: The five-lobed leaves in their smallest form measure one half to three quarters of an inch. In their largest form they grow to about one and one half inches long and almost two inches wide. The smallest leaves do resemble 'Meagheri'. The leaves are not as leathery as the leaves of 'Meagheri', but are smooth and satiny to the touch.

COLOR: A gay, bright green, with veins a lighter green describes the color of this plant.

HABIT OF GROWTH: 'Green Feather' has a neat habit of growth without ever getting straggly. Even when the vines are long, it keeps its neat look because the vines are so laden with leaves.

CULTURE: This plant is fairly hardy in areas south of New Jersey. Since I live just north of New York City, I bring all my potted ivies indoors in the winter except the hardiest of the hardy, such as baltica or '238th Street.'

Hedera Helix 'Fleur de Lis'

This is a most unusual ivy and one that is easy to identify by its name. The texture of the leaf is less leathery than most ivies and gives the plant a fragile, almost feminine look.

SIZE AND SHAPE: The terminal and two lateral lobes form a perfect fleur-de-lis. There are, however, two small basal lobes, but they are overpowered on most of the leaves by the size of the terminal and lateral lobes, and so the fleur-de-lis effect is not lost.

The lobes on this small-leafed ivy (one and one half inches) have such deep sinuses that with cursory examination one would be led to believe there are from three to five leaves coming from the same petiole. The terminal lobe is about an inch long and is usually twice the size of the lateral lobes and four times the size of the basal lobes.

COLOR: 'Fleur de Lis' is a delicate apple-green with a fragile network of veins that sometimes gives the leaf a mottled look. Petioles and vines are red.

HABIT OF GROWTH: Freely branching on graceful, slender vines, this plant is definitely a vining plant and should be grown as such.

CULTURE: Don't try growing this one outside. It's too good to risk losing. Find an important spot for it in a north or west window.

Hedera Helix 'Buttercup'

This is the yellowest of all ivies, but it is a far cry from the real buttercup color.

SIZE AND SHAPE: Take the color away and the shape is very close to Baltic, English, or 'Pittsburgh'. All lobes are sharply pronounced. The length of the terminal lobe is

almost the same as the width of the lateral lobes. The leaves are from three quarter inch to two inches.

COLOR: I obtained this ivy from a nursery whose catalogue described it as "freely suffused bright golden yellow." I have grown this plant in full sun, half sun and full shade and never, never have any of my plants been "freely suffused bright golden yellow." The sapling-green color of the leaf is certainly yellowish indeed, but it is rather like watered-down, colorless gelatin. Buttercup color, it is not.

HABIT OF GROWTH: It's a vigorous grower but is inclined to get long and straggly. Cut it back severely to make a compact plant. Don't forget to root your cuttings.

CULTURE: 'Buttercup' is hardy south of New York.

**Hedera Helix
'Erecta'**

This unique ivy is similar to 'Conglomerata' (page 129) and one of the best rock-garden specimens I know. It really does credit to its name, and once you've seen it you'll never forget it or confuse it with any other ivy. As its name implies, it grows upwardly erect, very reminiscent of a desert cactus.

'Erecta' can be trained to grow in the form you want if you guide it when it's young with a copper or galvanized wire. The stems, as they grow older, will grow thick, and when the wire is cut away the plant will stay in the shape to which it has been trained.

SIZE AND SHAPE: It is the shape of strength. The stout twigs and stems have very pointed leaves that are shaped like a triangle and rigidly arranged opposite each other. They remind me of the paper cut-out ladders children used to make. The three- to five-lobed leaves are very thick and leathery. The terminal lobe is long. The basal lobes are not strongly defined.

COLOR: 'Erecta' is a rich gray-green with pronounced gray veins.

HABIT OF GROWTH: 'Erecta' can rightly be called the maverick of the ivy family. Its branches grow upward as if in defiance of all its relatives. It is a very slow grower, but if you have the heart to cut a stem, it would give a strong accent in a "line" flower arrangement. However, before you cut a stem remember that it will take your plant considerable time to grow another stem as long.

The largest plant I've seen is two feet tall. Mine is about one and one half feet and is the senior ivy citizen of my plant room.

CULTURE: As long as it is not exposed to the drying wind of winter, it can be grown outdoors all year round as far north as New York. It loves plenty of moisture but needs good drainage.

Hedera Helix 'Conglomerata'

This is a most decorative ivy and reminiscent of a bonzai form. It does not have the familiar grace and flow of most ivies, but it has an exquisite style all its own. It would be right at home in a garden in Japan or in any formal setting. It can be used with dramatic effect in a dish garden on your coffee table.

'Conglomerata' is a close relative of *Hedera helix* 'Erecta,' and like this plant, it has a stiff habit of growth. Don't let its modern look fool you. It is not a new sport.

The *London Gardener's Chronicle*, back in June 1871, referred to it as the "new Ivy" shown by the Royal Horticultural Society.

SIZE AND SHAPE: The branches are stiff and mostly erect. The effect is completely modern. The three- to five-lobed leaves, crinkly and curled, cluster together so tightly that the look is almost contorted. The lateral lobe is often missing. The terminal lobe is rounded and the sinuses wide. Its stems grow upward like candles on a Christmas tree.

COLOR: 'Conglomerata' is a dark, dull green and quite beautiful in its matted sheen. The veins are very pronounced and gray.

HABIT OF GROWTH: Dwarf in form, the plant does not climb but rather strikes a pose. I have one that resembles an oriental dancer. For a striking effect, silhouette it against a white rock in your garden.

CULTURE: If you're going to grow it indoors, put it where it will receive plenty of light and don't forget to give it a weekly dousing. It's tougher than it looks and can be planted outdoors even in the Northeast United States.

14.
Starter's
Collection

Miniature	'JUBILEE'
Heart Shape	'SWEETHEART'
Fans	'CALIFORNIA FAN'
Bird's Foot	'IRISH LACE' 'ITSY BITSY'
Variegateds	'GOLDHEART'
Curlies	'MANDA'S CRESTED'
Ivy-Ivies	'GARLAND'
Oddities	'CONGLOMERATA'

15.
"Ivy" That Isn't Ivy

THERE ARE many plants that are called "ivy" but are not. These "ivies" include, among others:

Grape Ivy (*Cissus rhombifolia*)
Devil's Ivy or Pothos (*Scindapsus aureus*)
German or Parlor Ivy (*Senecio mikanioides*)
Kenilworth Ivy (*Cymbalaria muralis*)
Kangaroo Ivy (*Cissus antarctica*)
Boston or Japanese Ivy (*Parthenocissus tricuspidata*)
Poison Ivy (*Rhus radicans*)

Most of these make very good house plants (with the exception of Poison Ivy), but they are not members of the *Hedera* family or even remotely related. Some are very similar in appearance to real ivy, and for that reason they are included in this book so that you won't confuse them with the real thing.

Grape Ivy

This plant has bright olive-green foliage with bronze tones. The shiny three-part leaves are shaped like the leaves on Poison Ivy and are light to dark olive green with the bronze tint on the new growth. The underside of the leaves, as well as the younger stems, are covered with a fuzz of tiny, soft brown hairs. Its soil must be kept moist but not soaked. Grape Ivy is a native of South America.

Devil's Ivy or Pothos

This plant is often confused with Philodendron because the leaf shape is very similar. A native of the South Pacific Islands, it has heart-shaped leaves from two to four inches in length. Some leaves are marbled with pure white, while others show streaks of cream or yellow. Some are pure green. If kept in a dark location their coloring will become somewhat subdued with some leaves becoming completely green. Devil's Ivy is practically indestructible, but given adequate light and the privilege of drying out between waterings, it will respond with a colorful growth that most house plants cannot surpass.

German or Parlor Ivy

A native of South Africa, believe it or not, German Ivy is sometimes mistaken for *Hedera* because its leaves are similar in shape, but their color is a brighter green. The coarsely toothed leaves grow on a viny stem and trails or climbs. Mature plants form clusters of small, bright yellow flowers. They grow very fast and must be tip-pruned regularly for a compact house plant.

Kenilworth Ivy

This plant is a creeper with kidney-shaped, irregularly lobed leaves with shallow scallops on their edges. The miniature lilac-blue–snapdragon-type flowers have yellow throats. It's a native of the Alps and grows wild in the Appalachian mountains. Kenilworth Ivy is great for hanging baskets. New plants are easily grown because it is a creeper and roots wherever it touches moist ground.

Kangaroo Ivy

This "ivy" is an elegant trailing vine with large, shiny, saw-toothed leaves often six inches in length and shaped like an elm leaf. It does not grow too rapidly and needs cool temperatures.

Boston or Japanese Ivy

Many homes that seem to be covered with ivy in summer are really covered with Boston Ivy. This "ivy" is not a member of the *Hedera* family. It is a deciduous vine and makes a perfectly magnificent wall cover. Boston Ivy is vigorous and quick growing with large shiny grass-green leaves from two to seven inches wide. The leaves turn red and orange in autumn and can look spectacular against a wall.

Poison Ivy

I resent that this villainous plant has been given the name "Ivy." It is a shrub that crawls and climbs by means of aerial rootlets. The leaves consist of three somewhat oval, pointed leaflets, glossy on top and slightly hairy beneath. It has small greenish flowers that are followed by small, grayish round fruits, which remain on the plant all winter. In the fall the foliage turns red and orange. It should always be observed at as great a distance as possible. The extreme itching, burning, and blistering of the skin caused by the plant's toxicity can not only be painful but sometimes fatal.

THESE GOOD-LOOKING TREES OF HARDY OUTDOOR IVY ARE
EXAMPLES OF HOW ATTRACTIVE SIMPLE TOPIARY DESIGN CAN BE.

16.
Topiary –
Fun and Art

It used to be that only very rich people had topiaries. This art of training and cutting plant material into living sculptures has been practiced by the gardeners of wealthy landowners all over the world for centuries, perhaps since the Middle Ages.

In the formal gardens during the seventeenth and eighteenth centuries, gardeners outdid themselves in shaping symbolic and geometric masterpieces out of trees and bushes. Boxwood, Privet, and Yew were the materials most used. Still in existence at Earl's Hall in Fife, Scotland, is a fifteenth-century garden where a two-acre grove of twenty-foot-tall topiary yew trees are trimmed to resemble chess pieces. No one knows exactly when the topiaries were created, but their growth indicates that the impeccably cared for knights, kings, queens, and pawns are at least three centuries old.

There are many classic geometric and zoological examples to be found in the great gardens and arboreta of

Europe, the Orient, on our Pacific Coast, and in the public gardens at Colonial Williamsburg. Many of them are very old, and many of those I have seen are truly magnificent.

One drawback to these masterpieces is the length of time they take to complete—some five, ten years, others much longer. Then someone came up with the brilliant idea of using ivy, and now we have almost instant topiary. If you use a bushelful of ivy cuttings you can fashion a completed topiary in a day. Even if you don't, you can create a showpiece ivy topiary in just a few weeks or a few months depending upon the design. And you don't have to have a gardener to make it for you. In recent years, topiaries made with ivy have become a popular and rewarding pastime for the not-so-very rich as well as for the very rich.

Mrs. Colby Chester, a blue-ribbon topiary winner, tells of finding one in Portland, Oregon, and describes it as one of the most whimsical and ingenious topiaries she has ever seen.

It was in front of a small home nestled at the foot of Mount Hood. There stood a 20-foot-wide stump of a large and long since dead tree, too big to remove without great expense. The owner had carefully and cleverly planted a profusion of fast-growing common Ivy around its base, and then fashioned ears, nose and outstretched forepaws to create a startlingly realistic, environmentally appropriate, topiary bear!

The topiary forms you can buy are mostly portable and come in a variety of forms—animals, birds, cones, umbrellas, globes, pyramids, baskets. The selection is simply marvelous. However, they are not inexpensive although

(Photo by Spaeth.)

I have found some twenty-inch-high animal forms for as little as $9. The big spectacular forms run as high as $160, and you can get everything from a turtle to a nine-foot-tall grazing giraffe. Of course, it is possible to make your own portable plant sculpure, and this is not only fun but will be a test of your own imagination, ingenuity, and dexterity.

When To Start

You can start a topiary any time of the year. They do well indoors under Gro-lux lights. If you don't have artificial lights, keep your topiary in an east or west window. I like starting them in spring so they will be ready to set outdoors in a semi-shady spot during the summer.

Materials Needed

Galvanized or aluminum
  wire
Chicken wire
Coarse Sphagnum moss
Adhesive, electrical, or
  bicycle tape
Flexible, nonrust wire

Hairpins
Cotton-covered wire (avail-
  able at Dennisons, in
  New York)
Wire cutter
Wire bender (optional)

How To Make

There are two ways to make a topiary. You can plant
the ivy in a pot and train it up a frame that you anchor
in the *pot*. Or you can make a hollow frame and plant the
ivy in the *frame*. Thus the frame becomes the growing
container.

In both cases the frame must be sturdy. Use the heaviest
gauge of galvanized or aluminum wire you can handle.
Anything lighter than number 8 wire will lack rigidity.
I prefer aluminum because it is more flexible and lighter to
handle than galvanized. Galvanized wire eventually rusts,
aluminum does not.

IVY RING: For a beginner, the ivy ring is probably the
easiest. Simply cut a length of aluminum or galvanized
wire and anchor each end into a pot of soil. Put two
plants at opposite ends of the ring and train the vines to
grow up around the ring. As the vines grow, fasten them
with cotton-covered wire, and soon you'll have a thick,
lush green ring of ivy. This makes a wonderful center-

piece. You can hang ornaments, ribbons, all kinds of small seasonal decorations around the ring to make holiday parties gayer than ever.

IVY SPIRAL: This is a beauty and not very difficult to make. Get a strong stake (the kind you use for tomato plants). Cut it to the length you want your finished topiary, keeping in mind that part of it must go to the bottom of your pot or container. Put the stake into the soil so that it stands firmly. Hammer a nail into the top of the stake to use as an anchor for your wire. Fasten the end of the wire around the base of the wooden stake and shape spiral, making it widest at the bottom. Leave enough space between spirals to show a clear definition

when the ivy has grown up and around it. Hook the top end of wire around the nail. Train the ivy to grow up the spiral to the top, fastening whenever needed with cotton-covered wire.

IVY UMBRELLA: Another inexpensive and very effective instant topiary is one that resembles an umbrella. For this you need a tomato stake and a wire hanging-basket, which you can buy inexpensively at any garden center. Wrap wires of basket with wet, coarse sphagnum moss, tying it in place with flexible wire. (Wet sphagnum is easier to handle.)

Anchor the stake firmly in the soil in the middle of the pot and nail the basket, inverted, to the top. Train your

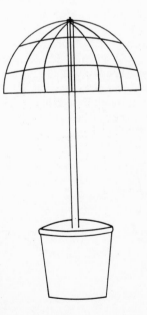

ivy to grow up and around the stake and around the sphagnum-covered wires of the basket. When it gets to the top, be sure to keep the leaves well sprayed with water.

Making a Frame for a Topiary

When you're ready to try making your own animal frame, I think you'll find a turtle form the easiest. Now mind you, I didn't say "easy." I said "easiest." If you can make this one, I believe you can make most of the others whether it's a beast, bird, or geometric form. Once you get the hang of it, it isn't difficult. It just takes imagination and dexterity.

First thing you do is make a pattern out of a large piece of paper of the shape of the turtle's bottom including his four legs and tail. In other words, the shape is the imprint a turtle would leave had he been lying on sand. Be certain the form is large enough so that the shape will be easily recognized and the details apparent when it is covered with ivy. The ivy will add more to the girth than to the length and can obscure whatever little details you might have had in mind. Remember, too, that if the *form* is of normal size, the finished creature will be too fat.

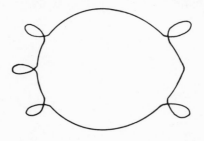

Place the wire around your pattern, making large loops for the legs and a small loop for the tail. (Head comes later.) Cut the wire with pliers. Bend ends so they can hook to each other. Now tape hooks tightly together with adhesive, electric, or bicycle tape. Cut a piece of wire long enough to go across (width) the turtle's back to form an arch.

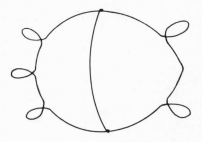

For the head, cut a length of wire to go lengthwise from tail to head—long enough to shape neck and head and return to tail. Hook at tail and tape at all junctures.

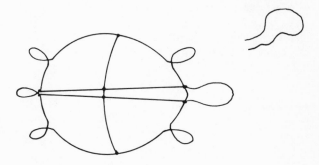

Cut two lengths of wire so that they reach from the tail to each side of the neck to form an arch. Hook the ends to the frame. Tape at all hooks and juncture points. (*Step A*)

Cut additional wires (two or more, depending on turtle size) to go across width of back. Hook and tape. (*Step B*)

Cut additional wires to go lengthwise from tail to base of neck, and weave them in and out of the width wires to give added strength to the superstructure. Hook and

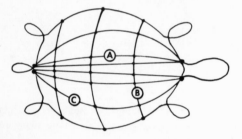

Now cut a wire to arch across (width) the head and back again. Hook and tape. Cut another wire to arch across the length of head and back again. Hook and tape. You now have a superstructure for the head.

Cover the body with one large piece of chicken wire by placing your chicken wire under the body and bringing up the ends so they meet on top of the back. Squeeze chicken wire to shape. Leave the top of the back open for stuffing of the sphagnum moss.

Similarly cover each of the legs, tail, and head with chicken wire, leaving an opening in each. Secure chicken wire to frame with flexible nonrust wire at juncture points.

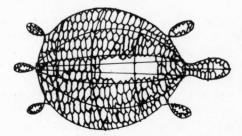

Another method to use when covering frame with chicken wire, especially when your topiary form is not a large one, is to cut strips of the chicken wire varying from three to six inches wide and curving them over the frame, one at a time. There will be some overlapping of sections, but you can obtain a smoother and cleaner shape than by squeezing large pieces of chicken wire over the frame. When using this method, don't forget to leave an opening to insert the sphagnum moss.

Sphagnum Moss

When the form is completed to your satisfaction, take as much coarse sphagnum moss as you think you'll need to stuff inside the frame. Soak it overnight in a solution of water and soluble fertilizer, such as Peters or Miracle-Gro. Drain for several hours, or if you're in a hurry, squeeze out the excess water. Now stuff the wet moss inside the chicken wire. It will take a while, but remember the tighter you pack the moss, the easier it will be to keep it moist.

Planting the Rooted Cuttings

Close the chicken wire on top of the body, head, tail, and feet as smoothly as possible by tying the ends together with flexible rust-proof wire, cutting away any excess chicken wire. The smoother the chicken wire, the better the finished configuration.

Now plant your cuttings directly into the moss and as close together as possible as the number of your cuttings will allow. Use a thick stick or pencil to firmly set in the roots. Short cuttings, about four inches long, are best. When the planting is finished, the topiary will have a scraggly appearance. To smooth it out, attach the trailing vines to the body with hairpins. The bare spots will soon fill in.

Topiary Care

Each day spray your forms thoroughly with a fine mist. Water the entire topiary at least twice a week so that the sphagnum is kept constantly moist. Feed with a water-soluble fertilizer once a month, using the fertilizer solution to spray the leaves as well as pouring it on to the roots. As the ivy fills in, clip it to conform with the design you had in mind.

When choosing a topiary remember that the larger

forms look the most exciting, but because of their size are not as easily sprayed and watered indoors. Put your topiary on a large saucer or some kind of receptacle to catch the water drippings, otherwise you'll ruin the floor under it. It's not easy to find a large saucer or container to hold the larger topiaries. My topiary turtle—almost a yard long from head to tail—was made in the spring and grown outdoors. When winter came and I brought it indoors, everytime I watered it, I had a floor to mop.

After a long search, I finally found at my garden center a rubber saucer about a yard in diameter. I put marble chips in it, rested the turtle on the chips, and not only did the saucer catch the dripping, but the water that fell on to the chips gave the topiary extra humidity.

A smart thing to do with indoor topiaries is to keep a sprayer nearby. Everytime you pass, it's easy to give them a spray. Human nature being what it is, the chore of spraying regularly may often be forgotten. With a sprayer near a topiary, you'll use it more regularly. Topiaries are prima donnas and won't take procrastination with the watering.

You don't have to spend a lot of money on sprayers. Just save the empty spray bottles that many household cleaning fluids come in, such as Fantastic and Windex.

Insects

Watch out for insects during winter months, especially if the room atmosphere is too dry. Isotox is a relatively safe spray to use indoors. If you need a fungicide, use Phalton. Many topi-buffs spray Phalton periodically as a precaution. I never needed it, and hopefully you won't either.

Your topiary will, with regular watering and feeding,

keep in prime condition for two or three years. After that the stems become woody and it becomes increasingly difficult to maintain the form's sleek appearance. The only solution is to rip out the ivy and start your fun all over again.

Some Ivies To Use for Topiaries

'Ivalace'	'Meagheri'
'Needlepoint'	'Glacier'
'Shamrock'	'Itsy Bitsy'

Other Topiary Suggestions

IVY WREATH: Another effective use of the topiary form, and one that can be kept in readiness in the garden, greenhouse, or in the cellar under lights until needed, is the ivy wreath. This can be used to frame punch bowls, centerpieces, or even candlesticks, depending upon the size you make.

Simply cut a circle of wood of any desired diameter

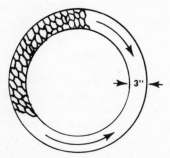

so that the rim is about three inches wide. Lay moistened and fertilized sphagnum moss on top of the circle and cover with chicken wire. Staple chicken wire to wood circle. Plant ivy cuttings and anchor with flexible wire.

You can make other variations using the wood base but in various shapes such as a Hogarth curve (S-shaped), triangles, or cut to look like a long garland running the length of your dining table. Once you have your fully grown form you can place seasonal decorations in and around it or put cut flowers into it.

IVY BALL: You will need two wire-hanging baskets and at least six plants with long vines for each basket, or as many rooted cuttings as required. The more you use, the fuller your ball. (All plants must be of the same ivy variety.)

Put ivy upside down in the empty basket so that all leaves and vines protrude through wire of basket. Then line basket completely with wet sphagnum moss. Pack good potting soil around roots of plant and up to brim of basket. Do the same thing with the other basket.

Place the two baskets together so their rims fit flush.

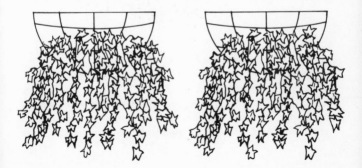

In order to prevent soil from spilling out when placing the two basket rims together, put a large, brown paper bag over the top of the basket before turning it upside down, then pull bag out when the two rims are together.

Fasten both rims with wire to hold them together. Now anchor the ivy vines to the ball with hairpins and presto —a topiary. Hang from top with a long piece of wire with a hook on the end.

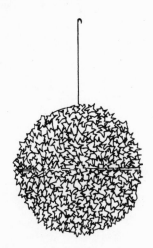

IVY BALL TREE: If you don't want to use the ivy ball hanging like a giant Christmas ornament, make a tree out of it. It's easy, and if you make two of them, you'll have a wonderful pair of ivy trees to adorn your front entrance.

Simply take three full-length tomato stakes and wire them together. Wrap this pole with wet sphagnum and tie it with flexible nonrust wire. Put pole in ten- or twelve-inch pot with soil. Place your ivy ball on top of pole and push it into the pole until it is secure, then nail it to the top of the stakes.

Plant three or four ivy plants at base of pole, and train them to grow up to reach the ivy ball.

Suppliers

Nurseries which specialize in Ivy

Merry Gardens, Camden, Maine, 04843
The Garden Spot, 4032 Rosewood Drive, Columbia,
South Carolina, 29205

Nurseries which also offer Ivy

Carroll Gardens, Westminster, Maryland, 21157
Logee's Greenhouses, Danielson, Connecticut, 06239
Mellinger's Inc., 2310 W.S. Range Road, North Lima,
Ohio 44452
The Tingle Nursery Co., Pittsville, Maryland, 21850

Wholesale nurseries which offer a few varieties

Baier Lustgarten, Jericho Turnpike, Middle Island,
New York, 11953
Mitsch Nursery, Route 2, Box 34, Aurora, Oregon, 97002

The American Ivy Society is helpful in supplying information about Ivy:

The American Ivy Society
128 West 58th Street
New York, New York, 10019

Index

Abundance, 63, 64, 65
Adult stage, 23
Aerial rootlets, 23
American Ivy Society, 156
Anthracnose, 20
Aphids, 20
Araliaceae, 22
Axil, 29

Baby English, 104
Bacchus, 6, 7, 8, 96
Balanced fertilizer, 15
Baltica, 24, 94, 111, 112, 124
Basal lobe, 28
Bates, Alfred, 121
Big Deal, 119, 120
Bird's Foot Ivy, 30
    Caenwoodiana, 33
    Irish Lace, 38, 39, 40, 131
    Itsy Bitsy, 40, 41, 131, 152
    Pedata, 24, 31, 32
    Plume D'or, 40
    Sagittaefolia, 42, 43

Shamrock, 35, 36, 37, 152
Shannon, 33, 34, 35
Star, 37, 38
Boston Ivy, 134
Bud sport, 2
Buettner, Mrs. Otto, 56
Bunch, 94, 95
Buttercup, 125, 126
Byron, George Gordon,
    Lord, 5

Caenwoodiana, 33
California Fan, 45, 46, 131
California Gold, 77, 78
Canary Cream, 26
Canary Island Ivy, 25, 26
Carroll Gardens, 156
Chaucer, Geoffrey, 5
Chen-Osiris, 5
Chester, Mrs. Colby, 35, 138
Conglomerata, 24, 118, 128,
    129, 130, 131
Curlies, 52

159

Curlies (*cont.*)
  Abundance, 63, 64, 65
  Curlilocks, 54, 55, 61
  Fluffy Ruffles, 57, 58, 59
  Ivalace, 62, 63, 152
  Manda's Crested, 24, 56, 57, 58, 61
  Parsley Crested, 59, 60
  Ripples, 60, 61, 62
  Telecurl, 53, 54, 61
Curlilocks, 24, 52, 54, 55, 61
Cuttings
  tip, 21
  root, 21

Danker, Fred, 121
Dealbata, 79
Dentata, 26
Dentato-variegata, 26
Devil's Ivy, 133
Dickens, Charles, 5
Discolor, 79
Diseases, 19, 20
  anthracnose, 20
  leaf spot, 20

Edge flower bed, 115, 116
Egyptian name, 5
Elena, 64
English Ivy, 110, 125
Erecta, 24, 118, 127, 128, 129
Everett, Mr. T. H., 88
Exotica, pictorial cyclopaedia of exotic plants, 55, 121

Fan, 48, 49

Fans, 44
  California Fan, 45, 46, 131
  Fan, 48, 49
  Green Ripples, 46, 47
  Green Spear, 50, 51
  Pixie, 49, 50
Fertilizer, 15, 16
Fleur de Lis, 124, 125
Fluffy Ruffles, 57, 58, 59

Garland, 96, 97, 131
German Ivy, 133
Glacier, 70, 71, 152
Glymii, 87, 88
Goldust, 24, 68, 69
Goldheart, 24, 66, 68, 131
Graf, Alfred, 55, 121
Grape Ivy, 133
Green Feather, 123, 124
Green Quartz, 25
Green Ripples, 35, 44, 46, 47
Green Spear, 50, 51
Ground cover, 16

Hahn, Mr. Sylvan, 93
Hairs, 24, 27
Hardy Outdoor Ivy, 108
  Hedera helix, 24, 110, 113
  Hedera helix baltica, 24, 94, 111, 112
  Hedera helix hibernica, 110, 111
  Hedera helix Pittsburgh, 53, 93, 112, 125
  Hedera helix 238th Street, 88, 112

Heart Shapes, 82
  Glymii, 87, 88
  My Heart, 25, 85, 86
  238th Street, 88, 112
  Scutifolia, (cordata), 84
  Sweetheart, 83, 84, 131
Hedera canariensis, 23, 25, 26
Hedera colchica, 23, 26, 113
Hedera colchica dentata, 113
Hedera colchica Dentato-
  Variegata, 113
Hedera helix, 23, 24, 110, 111,
  112, 113
Hedera nepalensis, 23, 26, 27
Hedera rhombea, 23, 27
Heise-Denmark, 24, 66, 71, 72,
  73
Hibbard, Mr. Shirley, 73, 102
Hibernica, 24, 110, 111
Horace, 5
Howardi, 79
Humidity, 16, 17

Indoor screens, 12
Insects, 19, 20
  aphids, 20
  mites, 19
  red spider, 19
  scale, 19
Intermediate sport, 2
International Flower Show,
  35
International Geranium Society, 84
Irish, 94, 111
Irish Lace, 38, 39, 40, 131

Itsy Bitsy, 40, 41, 131, 152
Ivalace, 62, 63, 152
Ivy
  adult stage, 23
  aerial rootlets, 23
  cuttings from, 21
  diseases, 19-20
  fertilizer, 15-16
  hairs, 24, 27
  humidity and, 16-17
  insects and, 19-20
  juvenile stage, 22-23
  layering, 20-21
  light for, 18
  pH and, 14-15
  plant parts, 28-29
  propagation, 20-21
  root cuttings, 21
  self-branching, 24
  soil for, 14-15
  tip cuttings, 21
  topiary, 137-155
  uses
    edging, 115
    ground cover, 116
    hedge, 116
    swag of garland, 116, 117
  water for, 16-17
  when to cut back, 115
  when to plant, 115
Ivy hedge, 116
Ivy-Ivies, 90
  Bunch, 94, 95
  Garland, 96, 97, 131
  Maple Queen, 24, 92, 93,
    94

Ivy-Ivies (*cont.*)
   Merion Beauty, 24, 53, 91,
     92
   Woodsii, 95, 96

Japanese Ivy, 27, 132, 134
Jefferson, Thomas, 10
Jubilee, 105, 106, 107, 131
Juvenile stage, 22, 23

Kangaroo Ivy, 134
Keats, John, 5
Kenilworth Ivy, 134
Koch, Mrs. Carolyn, 84

Lateral lobe, 28
Layering, 20, 21
Leaf Shine, 101
Leaf spot, 20
Light, 18
Lime, 16
Limestone rock, 14
Little Diamond, 76, 77
Lobe, 28
Logee's Greenhouses, 156
London Gardener's Chron-
   icle, 130
Lustgarten, Baier, 156

Manda, W. A., 57
Manda's Crested, 24, 52, 56,
   57, 61, 131
Maple Queen, 24, 90, 92, 93,
   94
Marginata, 73, 74

Marginata Grandis, 73
   Major, 73
   Media, 74
   Minor, 74
   Rubra, 74
Margino-maculata, 26
Marmorata Elegans, 66, 79, 80
Meagheri, 24, 118, 121, 122,
   123, 152
Mellinger's Inc., 156
Merion Beauty, 24, 53, 91, 92
Merry Gardens, Maine, 40,
   123, 156
Michaels, Mrs. Arthur, 25
Midrib, 28
Miniatures, 98
   Jubilee, 105, 106, 107, 131
   Minima, 102, 103
   Spinozia, 101, 102
   Triloba, 100, 101
   Walthamensis, 24, 104, 105
Minima, 102, 103
Mites, 19
Mitsch Nursery, 156
Monstrosa, 60
Monticello, 10
My Heart, 85, 86

National Horticulture Maga-
   zine, 122
Needlepoint, 152
Nepal Ivy, 26
Nero, 1
New York Botanical Garden,
   88
Node, 29

Oddities, 118
  Big Deal, 119, 120
  Buttercup, 125, 126
  Conglomerata, 24, 129, 130, 131
  Erecta, 24, 127, 128, 129
  Fleur de Lis, 124, 125
  Green Feather, 123, 124
  Meagheri, 24, 121, 122, 123
  Small Deal, 120, 121
Old Garden, 46

Parasite, ivy as, 10
Parlor Ivy, 133
Parsley Crested, 59, 60
Peat Moss, 14
Pedata, 24, 30, 31, 32
Perlite, 14, 21
Persian Ivy, 26
Petiole, 29
pH, 14, 15
Pittsburgh, 53, 93, 112, 125
Pixie, 49, 50
Plants similar to ivy, 132
  Boston Ivy, 134
  Devil's Ivy, 133
  German Ivy, 133
  Grape Ivy, 133
  Japanese Ivy, 134
  Kangaroo Ivy, 134
  Kenilworth Ivy, 134
  Parlor Ivy, 133
  Poison Ivy, 135
  Pothos, 133
Pliny the Elder, 6
Plume D'or, 40

Poison Ivy, 135
Pothos, 133
Propagation, 20, 21

Rays, 24, 27
Red spider, 19
Ripples, 60, 61, 62
Root cuttings, 21
Ross, Mary Ellen, 123
Royal Horticultural Society, 130

Sagittaefolia, 24, 42, 43
Sagitaefolia variegata, 80, 81
Scutifolia (cordata), 84
Self-branching ivies, 24
Scale, 19
Shakespeare, William, 5
Shamrock, 35, 36, 37, 152
Shannon, 33, 34, 35
Sinus, 29
Small Deal, 120, 121
Smith, Captain John, 10
Soil, 14, 15
Spaghnum, milled, 14
Spinozia, 101, 102
Sports, 1, 2
Star, 37, 38
Sub Marginata, 74, 75, 76
Sweetheart, 83, 84, 131

Telecurl, 24, 52, 53, 54, 57, 61
Terminal lobe, 28
Tingle Nursery, 156
Tip cuttings, 21

Topiary, 137-155
  care of, 150
  forms, 142
    ball, 153
    ball tree, 154
    ready-made, 138, 143
    ring, 143
    spiral, 144
    umbrella, 145
    wreath, 152
  history, 137
  how to make, 142, 146
  insects, and, 151
  ivies to be used, 141
  materials needed for, 142
  when to start, 142
Triloba, 100, 101
238th Street, 88, 112

Variegateds, 66

California Gold, 77, 78
Glacier, 70, 71, 152
Goldheart, 25, 68, 131
Goldust, 25, 68, 69
Heise-Denmark, 25, 71, 72, 73
Little Diamond, 76, 77
Marginata, 73, 74
Marmorata Elegans, 79, 80
Sagittaefolia, 24, 80, 81
Sub Marginata, 74, 75, 76
Vermiculite, 14,
Vergil, 5, 6

Walthamensis, 24, 98, 104, 105
Water, 16, 17
Weber's California, 77
Woodsii, 95, 96
Wordsworth, William, 5